C000170877

Housing Finance

a basic guide

Peter Malpass
and
Henry Aughton

Fifth revised edition

Shelter

Fifth revised edition (First edition published in 1981)
Published in 1999 by Shelter, 88 Old Street, London EC1V 9HU
Registered Company 1038133
Registered Charity 263710

British Library Cataloguing-in-Publication Data – a catalogue
record for this book is available from the British Library.

ISBN 1 870767 75 6

Illustrations by Bob Dewar
Editing and layout by Rahila Gupta, London NW2 4BH
Printed by Stanley L Hunt, Northamptonshire, NN10 9UA
Trade Distribution by Turnaround Publishing Services

Acknowledgements

Henry Aughton wrote the first two editions of Housing Finance and did most of the work on the third edition. It is impossible to overstate the importance of Henry's contribution, beginning with the first edition in 1981 at a time when there was nothing else available for readers who wanted a simple and straightforward explanation of housing finance in Britain. My role has been to try to carry forward the spirit of Henry's approach and to produce new editions which keep the Basic Guide both readable and up to date.

In producing this fifth edition I have been supported by Imogen Wilson and Rosemary Bourke at Shelter, and by Rahila Gupta who edited the draft into a publishable form. I am also grateful to Kat Harris for the worked examples of benefit claims in chapter 5, and to Rita Diaz for checking the accuracy of the statistics throughout the book. Thanks are due to Henry Aughton for reading and commenting on the first redraft of the full text.

I must add, of course, that none of these people bears any responsibility for any errors that remain.

Peter Malpass
Bristol
May 1999

Note about the authors

Peter Malpass is Professor of Housing Policy at the University of the West of England, Bristol. He has been involved in housing since 1970, initially as a door-to-door council rent collector but mainly as a teacher and researcher. He has published widely on many aspects of housing and housing policy; he is the co-author (with Alan Murie) of *Housing Policy and Practice* (now in its fifth edition), and he has recently finished work on the first full length historical account of housing associations and housing policy in Britain, which is due to be published by Macmillan in 2000.

Henry Aughton has a background in both housing and finance. He was Hemel Hempstead's Borough Treasurer for 14 years and subsequently Dacorum District Council's first Chief Executive. Altogether he has had 47 years' experience in local government. He was adviser to the Association of Municipal Corporations and specialist adviser in 1977 and 1978 to the House of Commons Environment Sub-Committee. He also served on working parties of the Chartered Institute of Public Finance and Accountancy and was, for many years, Deputy Chair of Shelter and Chair of its finance committee.

Contents

List of Tables and Figures

Tables

Figures

1 Overview

Housing finance is widely regarded as a difficult, technical subject, best left to accountants and other experts in the field. In fact, of course, it is too important to be ignored by non-specialists. This book is designed to introduce and explain the basics of housing finance in a straightforward way for people who need to know how things work but who do not want to go into too much detail. Housing finance is a fast-moving policy area, and important changes seem to follow quickly one after the other. For example, over the last ten years we have seen major reforms in the arrangements affecting rents and subsidies, as well as the phasing out of mortgage interest tax relief. However, further fundamental changes are in prospect, including local authority housing accounts and the reform of housing benefit. In these circumstances it is important to have a good grasp of the basic principles, for then it is much easier to understand the changes and their likely impact. The aim of the book, therefore, is to provide an account of how the system works now, and how it might develop in the foreseeable future. The scope of the book is limited to England and Wales; much of what follows is applicable in Scotland and Northern Ireland but, in certain respects, the situation and the legislation in these parts of the United Kingdom is different.

What is housing finance?

In simple terms there are two sides to housing finance – the ways in which the production of new housing (and the refurbishment of existing dwellings) is financed, and the ways that households pay for their accommodation. These two aspects can be referred to as production and consumption finance. There are various ways of raising the large amounts of money required to produce new dwellings, and of helping households pay for something which they must have but, in most cases, cannot afford to pay for outright. The British housing system is usually discussed in terms of four main categories:

- *owner-occupation (66.9 per cent)*

- *council housing (18.7 per cent)*

- *private renting (9.8 per cent)*

- *registered social landlords (RSLs) – mostly housing associations (4.6 per cent)*

These four categories are referred to as 'tenures', a label describing the terms on which households occupy their homes. Each of the four main tenures is associated with its own distinctive financial framework. The structure of this book reflects this way of thinking and different chapters look at the financial arrangements within each of the main tenures.

There are more than 24 million dwellings in Great Britain. The total grows by less than one per cent per annum, and most of the huge amount of money spent on housing each year is devoted to paying for dwellings that already exist. From the point of view of individual households, housing costs (rent or mortgage repayments) generally constitute the largest single item of regular expenditure. But for governments, too, housing is an important element of public expenditure, although not anything like as significant as health or education. Total public expenditure on housing in England in 1998-99 amounted to more than £11.7 billion, including the £6.1 billion cost of housing benefit for private and housing association tenants, which appears in the social security budget. To understand housing finance, therefore, we have to look at how households pay for housing and at how governments raise and spend money; this requires some recognition of the way that housing expenditure fits into and is constrained by governments' attempts to control public expenditure and to manage the economy as a whole.

In terms of the big picture, expenditure on housing production and consumption has a significant influence on the state of the wider economy. Governments cannot afford to ignore what is happening in the housing market. Indeed they sometimes try to use the housing market as a lever to influence the wider economy.

Housing – special features

Two particular characteristics are important for an understanding of housing finance. First, housing is very expensive to produce – because it requires land, considerable amounts of materials and many hours of labour time. The high cost of housing has led to the development of ways of allowing people to spread the cost of their housing over long periods. Renting and mortgaged house purchase developed as different ways of allowing them to do so. Another way of dealing with the high cost of housing is to provide a subsidy of some kind, and much of the debate about housing finance revolves around this issue.

The second key feature is that housing is what economists call a durable commodity, unlike for example food and drink, or semi-durable commodities like cars or washing machines. Its length of life – for practical purposes only land has a longer life – makes it almost unique. The long life of houses means that they retain their value over many years. The effect of inflation is particularly important because, over a period of time, the value of houses in money terms actually grows. It is for this reason that housing has come to be seen as a good investment. Over the last 30 years the growth in house prices has been spectacular, even allowing for the falls that were witnessed in the early 1990s.

There are other factors besides inflation which affect house prices. There is the availability or scarcity of mortgage funds from building societies and banks, or the sudden variations of mortgage interest rates. The scarcity of affordable rented property in many areas increases the pressure on house prices by obliging numbers of people to buy, even when, on any rational view, they cannot really afford it.

The steady pressure of demand for housing, whether for renting or buying, should in theory produce increased supply. In this way the market, operating freely, is supposed to solve the problem. Unfortunately housing demonstrates another unhelpful characteristic - in the short term supply is 'inelastic', i.e. it cannot be increased rapidly, simply because of the time taken to build each house. Because of the long timescale of production, prudent builders will only increase supply if they are sure that there will still be adequate demand when the houses are ready. Whatever the demand, the size of the housing stock grows only slowly. To increase the total supply by two per cent per annum would require the production of 460,000 dwellings, a figure not even approached in Britain for more than 30 years.

Ever since the First World War, it has been accepted that decent housing standards are an essential condition of a just and healthy society, and are as necessary in an advanced industrial society as effective health, education and welfare services. There was, for much of the period since 1945, a national consensus about this, although different parties attached different emphasis at times to various aspects of housing policies. Unfortunately housing is such a significant element in terms of the resources it requires that governments have often used housing policies as tools in their overall management of the nation's economy.

Visible and invisible subsidies

Over the years housing has been subsidised in various ways. There has been much debate about what counts as housing subsidy and how it should be measured. Most economists prefer to define subsidy as the difference between the price actually charged for an item and the price that it would fetch in a free market. But this can be difficult to measure, because where the market is not completely free (as has been the case in housing since 1915) no one can confidently say what that price would be. In practice, the debate about housing subsidies has concentrated on a 'cash flow' approach. In council housing this means the amount of money that is provided to make up the difference between the rents charged and the amount necessary to cover expenditure on the housing service.

In Britain, the cost of subsidies to council housing has been a constant topic for government ministers. The cost of subsidising home-ownership, on the other hand, was seldom mentioned. It is only within the last 25 years that it has become widely understood that home-owners are subsidised. The Treasury maintained for many years that tax relief was not a subsidy. It suited them to argue that a subsidy is an actual payment, whereas this was tax foregone – how could it be a subsidy not to take someone's own money away from them? This is very reassuring until it is realised that the effect is precisely the same. The payment of a subsidy increases the disposable income of the fortunate recipient; and so does tax relief.

How it looks to economists

Academic economists point to two features of housing – the investment aspect, which is involved in the provision of a dwelling; and the consumption aspect, which is the use and benefit of the accommodation.

With private rented housing, as with council housing, the landlord bears the cost of provision. This investment results in ownership of an asset which will produce an income, the rent, paid by the tenant. The landlord has the ownership, the tenant has the use.

In considering what the rent should be, economists tend to favour market rents, or something close to market rents. The rental value of a dwelling is what people are prepared to pay for the use of it, irrespective of what it cost the owner to acquire it. Scarcity of rented accommodation will result in higher rents unless there is interference with market forces by rent control. In the view of economists, this is as it should be, for higher rents will eventually increase supply. They contend that where a tenant pays a lower rent, the subsidy is the amount of the difference between the market rent and rent actually paid, and it is a subsidy borne by the landlord.

There are, however, landlords who have not been concerned with profit, nor with the strictures of market theory. They are local authorities and housing associations, and nowadays they provide more than twice as many rented dwellings as do the private landlords. Their purpose has always been to meet the housing needs of people who can afford neither to buy nor to pay the sort of rent which a free market would require. Affordable rents may not provide sufficient income to cover the cost of borrowing, and of management and maintenance. Hence there is a need for housing subsidies, whether in the form of annual payments towards the upkeep, or payments towards the initial cost of provision.

Central government and housing finance

Governments have always needed to know how much they have to raise to meet the calls that would be made on them. In modern times governments have also found themselves attempting, with varying success, to manage the economy. In this they have been concerned, among other things, with the share of the total national income (the Gross Domestic Product, or GDP) which the public sector, national and local, will absorb. A large part of this sector's needs will be met by taxation and other revenues and the rest was referred to as the Public Sector Borrowing Requirement (PSBR), now replaced by Public Sector Net Borrowing (PSNB).

Each year a White Paper is published, called *The Government's Expenditure Plans*. This gives details of expenditure for each group of services (defence, social services, education, housing and so on) for the past five years and the current year, and what is planned for the next three years. The various tables cover local authority as well as central government activity. The White Paper became so big that the Government now produces it in a number of separate volumes; housing is dealt with in the volume titled the *Annual Report of the Department of Environment, Transport and the Regions.*

The mass of figures, analyses and supporting statements is intended to provide the basis on which the government's fiscal policy (how, and how much, is to be raised in taxes) and its borrowing requirement can be determined. It also gives the information needed for economic management.

Table 1 shows the main items of public expenditure on housing in the *Annual Report 1999.*

Table 1
Housing public expenditure in England, 1998-99 to 2001-02

£ million	1998-99 estimated outturn	1999-00 plans	2000-01 plans	2001-02 plans
Capital				
Housing Corporation				
Net ADP	735.1	789.9	757.2	686.2
Local Authority	1207.9	1252.3	1891.5	2380.3
Other	30.4	7.0	0.2	0.2
Total capital	1973.4	2049.2	2648.9	3066.7
Revenue				
Housing Corporation	201.3	199.7	183.5	188.0
Local authorities				
HRA subsidy	3,475.0	3,503.0	3,510.7	3,472.4
Other	22.4	9.1	57.3	157.3
Total revenue	3,698.7	3,711.8	3,751.5	3,817.7
Total	5,672.1	5,761.0	6,400.4	6,884.4

Table 1a
Local authorities capital expenditure

£ million	1998-99 estimated outturn	1999-00 plans	2000-01 plans	2001-02 plans
Basic credit approvals	383.8	451.8	1,819.6	2,305.4
Capital receipts initiative	570.2	570.2	0.0	0.0
Total credit approvals	954.0	1,022.0	1,819.6	2,305.4
Capital grants				
Private sector renewal	155.9	165.1	0.0	0.0
Disabled facilities grant	65.2	64.9	71.8	74.8
Total capital grants	221.1	230.0	71.8	74.8
Total	1,175.1	1,252.0	1,891.4	2,380.2

Table 1b
Local authorities revenue expenditure

£ million	1998-99 estimated outturn	1999-00 plans	2000-01 plans	2001-02 plans
HRA Subsidy				
Housing element				
Total deficit on housing element	551.1	534.0	505.0	483.0
Total surplus on housing element	-1,295.0	-1,382.0	-1,496.0	-1,579.0
Total of deficits and surpluses	-739.9	-848.0	-991.0	-1,096.0
Rent Rebate element				
Total cost of rebates	4,214.9	4,351.0	4,501.7	4,568.4
Net cost (total minus surpluses on housing element)	2,919.9	2,969.0	3,005.7	2,989.4
Total HRA subsidy	3,475.0	3,503.0	3,510.7	3,472.4

From 1992/93 to 1998/99 there was a steep decline in capital spending by local authorities and in the total amount of revenue subsidy to council housing. During this period capital expenditure by local authorities on housing fell by 60 per cent. However, in 1997/98 the newly elected Labour Government released the first tranche (£174 million) of capital receipts accumulated by councils from the sale of houses under the Right to Buy. This was followed by a further £610 million in 1998/99 (£570 million of this in England). The new Government's Comprehensive Spending Review was announced in July 1998. It envisaged a total of £3.6 billion additional spending by local authorities on housing over the next three years, plus £800 million for the New Deal for Communities which will include some money for housing. The additional money for housing investment is intended to be spent on the renovation of existing council dwellings rather than new building. As far as new building is concerned, the Government remains committed to the housing associations as the major providers. However, their Approved Development Programme has also suffered deep cuts (of 69 per cent) since the peak year of 1992/93, and expenditure is planned to decrease by 2001-02.

Up to 1992/93 local authority capital programmes always exceeded those of housing associations. Housing association capital expenditure is mostly used to pay for new building to add to the stock. Nowadays local authority capital expenditure is overwhelmingly used for renovation of the existing stock.

When comparing the figures for local authorities and housing associations, it is important to remember three key points. First, capital expenditure by the Housing Corporation is only a part of the total capital expenditure of housing associations. The private finance raised by

associations is not shown in the tables. In the case of local authorities, however, the whole of their capital programme counts as public expenditure, and therefore does appear in the tables.

Second, local authorities and housing associations are subsidised in different ways; the whole of the capital expenditure line for the Housing Corporation represents subsidy (social housing grant), paid as a lump sum at the time of construction. The figures for capital expenditure by local authorities on their own housing, however, refer to permission to borrow the necessary money. There is no subsidy element in these figures. Central government expenditure here (if any) comes in the form of revenue support towards the costs of repaying loans over a long period. This is included in the housing element of the HRA subsidy.

Third, while the figures for HRA subsidy include the cost of rent rebates (housing benefit) paid to council tenants, the housing public expenditure tables do not show the cost of housing benefit paid to housing association tenants. In their case the cost of housing benefit is included in the social security accounts (where it properly belongs).

One other glaring omission from the Housing Programme is any mention of the tax relief for owner-occupiers. It is now generally acknowledged that mortgage interest tax relief was a subsidy to house purchase, and that it was worth as much as £7.7 billion at its peak in 1990-91. The cost of this was never included in the programme totals although it was given reasonable prominence in a note that followed. This has been discontinued and annual reports make no reference at all to the subject. Mortgage interest relief was gradually reduced during the 1990s and abolished altogether in the Budget of March 1999 (with effect from April 2000).

2　Council Housing

Local authorities in Great Britain own more than four million dwellings, most of which were built between 1919 and 1979. For practical purposes, council housing did not exist until the responsibility of acting as the main providers of new rented housing was placed on the local authorities by the Housing and Town Planning Act, 1919. Until then a handful of charitable trusts and model dwellings companies (forerunners of the housing association movement) had built more houses than all the councils put together. Most councils had built no houses at all before 1914.

Other countries faced similar housing shortages in the aftermath of World War I, but they turned to their equivalent of housing associations. That choice was not open to Britain, whose housing associations were too few, too small and without the necessary financial muscle to deal effectively with the colossal tasks which this country faced in the wake of the First World War. The decision of that and every successive government until 1979, to place the responsibility for providing and managing rented housing on the local authorities, has been more than justified by their achievements.

Let us consider then, the financial framework within which councils operate as providers of housing. In this chapter, the next two sections look at the capital and revenue sides of housing finance, and make reference to the historical background; this is followed by a description of the current system and then proposals for changes to be introduced from April 2000 and 2001.

Providing the houses: the capital side

The distinction between capital and revenue is central to any understanding of housing finance, and yet it is a distinction that is sometimes quite hard to pin down. A convenient starting point is to think of capital expenditure as the initial cost of producing or acquiring an asset, such as a house, and revenue expenditure as the running costs arising from keeping the asset in use. For accounting purposes there is a convention that capital expenditure refers to items that have a long life, or at least a life that extends beyond a single accounting period (normally one year). Thus, expenditure on the creation of durable assets, such as houses or on major repairs (including roofs and windows) counts as capital, and this is normally financed by long-term borrowing, repayable over the life of the assets themselves. However, the costs of management and day-to-day maintenance count as revenue expenditure, and are funded by regular income, chiefly in the form of rents. The same kind of distinction can be made in any tenure, and so, for example, owner-occupiers usually finance the capital expenditure involved in buying their homes by taking out long-term loans, which they repay out of regular income. And, just like a local housing authority, when faced with decisions about how to pay for repairs they can choose to capitalise the costs (ie to spread them over time) or to meet them in full from current income.

Although local authorities no longer build new houses they continue to have major capital programmes of expenditure on their existing stock of dwellings. This will be of growing importance over the next few years as part of the Government's strategy for tackling urban regeneration and social exclusion. The balance between new building and renovation has changed over time, and so has the range of sources of capital funds. Historically, when councils began building houses they relied exclusively on borrowed money, repaid over 60 years. More recently, and especially since the introduction of the Right to Buy in 1980, councils have had capital receipts from the sale of assets. In the same period more and more councils came to make use of revenue contributions for capital outlay (RCCOs) – which means that they used surplus revenue income to cover part of the cost of projects that could have been financed by borrowing. Thus, there are three main sources of capital for investment in housing: borrowing, reserves and revenue.

In the case of projects funded by borrowing, the necessary loans are not raised directly from external lenders, and loans are not earmarked for particular projects. Local authorities need to borrow money on a regular basis in order to manage their affairs, to make sure that there is cash available when it is required to pay the wages of the staff and to pay other bills. This treasury function is carried out centrally by the finance department on behalf of the authority as a whole. Some loans will be long term (typically for periods of five to twenty-five years or even longer) while other borrowing will be for shorter periods. All borrowing is accounted for in a single Loans Fund, which raises money externally from financial institutions, the government's Public Works Loan Board, companies, and individuals. The Loans Fund then acts as an internal lender to whichever department needs to borrow for capital spending. This is a great accounting and administrative convenience, and has other important advantages. The Loans Fund will contain loans taken out at different times and at different rates of interest (some fixed and some variable), but the council is able to set an average rate of interest which will change only slightly each year. The method provides great stability.

The Loans Fund has to pay interest, of course, to all those from whom it has borrowed. It recharges this interest, at the average rate (the loans pool rate) to all the services which owe it money. Each year, it gets back from each of the services, including housing, the interest on the loans and an appropriate amount of repayment of principal. In this way the cost of capital projects can be spread (or amortised) over a very long period, 60 years, thereby minimising the annual burden of debt charges, while external loans can be for shorter periods. This separation between loans and the projects that they are designed to finance, and between loans and the rate at which debt is written off, is central to an understanding of the capital side of local authority housing finance.

Throughout the period, 1919-1979, local councils were building far more houses than they sold. Therefore, they relied on borrowing to fund their capital programmes. But since the introduction of the Right to Buy in 1980, sales have outstripped new building every year and capital receipts have become much more significant. The rules about the use of capital receipts have changed according to government spending priorities. During the 1980s an estimated £6 billion was accumulated by authorities, and some councils managed to spend all of their receipts. Since 1988 many councils have sold off the whole of their housing stock, thereby generating single large receipts. These have been used to repay debt, to pay for new town halls or swimming pools and to provide loans to the newly formed housing associations that now own the former council houses.

The funding of capital expenditure from revenue income has a long history, but until recent times it was as insignificant as funding from capital receipts. The main reason for this was simply that in the past, when council housing was young and expanding, the level of debt per dwelling was, in relative terms, much higher than it is today. At that time, all HRAs always showed big deficits before subsidy whereas now most are in surplus, so there is more cash available to contribute to capital expenditure. Another factor since 1990 has been restrictions on borrowing and the use of capital receipts, forcing more councils to look to revenue funding.

There is a further and much more recent way of funding capital projects, known as the Private Finance Initiative (PFI). This was invented in the early 1990s as a way of paying for necessary investment in public services but without the cost counting as public expenditure. It is based on the idea that if private developers borrow the capital necessary to build a school or hospital this is not defined as public expenditure, even though the building may be run as a state school or NHS hospital. Under the PFI developers provide buildings which are then leased to the public sector for an agreed period, and so the cost falling within the public accounts is just the annual sum payable on the lease. Initially housing was not eligible for PFI funding. But in 1998 the Government announced plans to set up pilot projects to enable councils to begin to use PFI resources for the refurbishment of their estates.

Government control of capital spending

Governments have always laid down rules about borrowing and the length of repayment periods, but until the mid-1970s there was little attempt to control the total amount of borrowing undertaken by any individual council. The number of houses any council chose to build was essentially for them to decide. Consent to borrow (called a loan sanction) had to be sought for each scheme. As long as this complied with government guidelines on building costs and standards, a loan sanction would not be refused, although it might be delayed in order not to breach total public expenditure plans for the year. Since 1976, however, a system of controls over the capital expenditure of individual authorities has been developed. Now each authority is given an annual Basic Credit Approval (BCA) covering the total amount of capital expenditure that it can finance from borrowing. This is discussed in more detail later in this chapter (see p24)

Paying for the houses: the revenue side

The running costs of council housing include management, repairs, loan charges and other items. This recurring revenue expenditure is met mainly from rents and Exchequer subsidies (including rent rebate subsidy). Until 1990, there could also be a contribution from councils' own tax income (the rates, now known as the council tax). This was compulsory if the housing revenue account would otherwise have been in deficit. The rules covering subsidies, rent setting arrangements and the treatment of revenue deficits or surpluses have changed considerably over the years. It would be confusing to go into too much detail here but it is necessary to say a bit about some basic principles. For instance, local authorities have always had (apart from 1972-74) freedom to set the rents of individual houses, and because of this freedom the Treasury has always sought ways of limiting its liability for subsidy. For 50 years up to 1972 this was achieved by paying subsidies as fixed cash sums per dwelling per year for a specified number of years.

In more recent times the approach has been to set subsidy in relation to notional Housing Revenue Account (HRA) deficits, determined by central government, irrespective of the actual rents set by local authorities. The HRA is a statutory account maintained by every local housing authority since 1936 to record all income and expenditure relating to dwellings provided under the various Housing Acts (councils that transfer their entire housing stocks to new landlords are not required to maintain HRAs). Authorities are expected to ensure that the account balances each year. It is important to be clear that this has always been interpreted to mean that councils only had to raise sufficient income to cover actual expenditure, and not to produce a given rate of return on the capital value of the stock. This can be defined as historic cost pricing as distinct from current value pricing which is practised in the private rented sector and which means that rents are set in relation to the current value of the property. Historic cost pricing has had the effect of helping to keep rents at affordable levels without unreasonably high levels of subsidy. However, as we shall see, the system is set to change in 2001, with far-reaching consequences.

Other key features of the system which have endured for many years are that rents are set at 'reasonable' levels, rather than by reference to the market or to individual capital values, and that local authorities have the freedom to practise rent pooling. This means that the rent of any one house is not tied to the costs of providing that particular dwelling. In other words, rent pooling is a form of averaging which enables councils to spread the costs of more recently built, and therefore more expensive, houses across the stock as a whole. Historically, rent pooling was used by governments as a way of dragging up the rents on older houses. By not increasing the subsidy on new houses in line with rising costs in the 1950s, governments could put pressure on councils to raise extra income by increasing the rents of older houses. This, in effect, moved the subsidy on these older houses over to the new ones, helping to keep their rents affordable.

Differences in rents from one authority to another were mainly due to differing land and building costs at the time when houses were built; local political influence was not generally a key factor. In the past critics tended to highlight differences in rents in apparently similar authorities next door to each other. However, the Conservative Governments in the late 1980s focused on what was seen as the *insufficient* variation in council rents from one region to another, especially when compared with the way that house prices varied across the country. Government policy since 1990 has been to widen differences in rents and to try to make these differences reflect the pattern of house price variation.

The Local Government and Housing Act, 1989

The current arrangements for both capital and revenue finance in local authority housing date from the Local Government and Housing Act, 1989, which took effect on 1 April 1990. When the Conservatives won the 1987 election they could look back on the great strides they had made. More than a million council houses had passed into owner-occupation. Council building for rent had reduced sharply to just 16,111 starts in 1988, while a million families remained on council waiting lists. Council building programmes suffered further cuts after 1989 and by 1992, completions were down to a derisory 4,085 in Great Britain as a whole. Housing subsidies, £1,423 million in 1980-81, had been cut to £409 million in 1985-86, and changes to the subsidy system, under the Housing Act, 1980, had resulted in massive rent increases, as intended. But in the Government's view, much still remained to be done, and a White Paper, *Housing: The Government's Proposals* (Cm 214, September 1987), set out the new plans.

The proportion of owner-occupation in Britain, one of the highest in the world, was to be expanded. Housing associations, together with private and commercial landlords, were to be the future providers of rented housing. Private landlords would have freedom to charge market rents for new lettings.

Council housing still dominated the rented market; but in the Government's view it was often not in the best interests of tenants. As the Government saw it, although management was good in some places, it was distant and bureaucratic in the big cities with poor maintenance performance in many areas. Ministers were critical of what they regarded as indiscriminate subsidy from the rates in some areas. According to them, whole communities had slipped into permanent dependency on the welfare state. Local authorities should therefore cease to provide housing, and would have an 'enabling' role in encouraging other landlords to make provision.

The White Paper said that council tenants must have more opportunity to control their own destinies including the right to choose other landlords. There were to be powers to set up housing action trusts (HATs) to renovate run-down council housing in the inner cities.

Some changes, including tenants' choice and HATs were introduced in the Housing Act, 1988. Further reform of housing finance was delayed until a second Bill was published in the autumn of 1988, following two consultation papers issued in July 1988. One was called *Capital Expenditure and Finance* and covered other services as well as housing; the other, *New Financial Regime for Local Authority Housing*, dealt with the housing revenue account, subsidies, rents and housing finance generally.

The capital finance system

In order to appreciate the need for reform it may help to outline the Government's criticisms of the system it introduced in 1980 and discontinued in April 1990. This system controlled the capital expenditure of councils and prescribed what this was: mainly acquisition and development of land, building work, vehicles, plant and machinery, housing repairs when the cost is met by borrowing, and capital grants and advances. Expenditure was authorised by the annual Housing Investment Programme (HIP), and the allocation was normally backed by borrowing approval. Repair work financed in any other way did not count as 'prescribed expenditure'. There was a ten per cent tolerance between years to allow for the carry-over of unspent allocations. Overspending was not illegal.

Capital receipts (mainly from the sale of council houses) could also be used, though only 20 per cent could be used for 'prescribed' expenditure (eg for new building) in the year that the council received the money. Twenty per cent of any remaining receipts could be used the next year and so on. Thus, over a period of years this 'cascade' effect permitted virtually the whole amount to be spent. In addition, councils could use receipts for 'non-prescribed' expenditure (this allowed them to renovate their existing stock). Local authorities made good use of their powers to use capital receipts – they could build and repair without having to borrow (which would have used up scarce borrowing permission). The right to carry forward unspent capital receipts was seen by housing authorities as natural. It was their money arising from the sale of their property. But the Government saw the cascade effect as a danger; they wanted the bulk of receipts to be used to pay off existing debts.

The new system introduced in 1990 set out to control borrowing, instead of expenditure. It applies to the financing of any capital expenditure not met from revenue, and uses the term, credit arrangement, to cover borrowing and its equivalent. The definition of what constitutes capital expenditure is wider than before. For example, it includes 'enhancement' which is anything that substantially lengthens the life of an asset (as distinct from repair which merely restores it to its original state), increases its market value, or increases the extent to which it can be used.

Each year the DoE (now the DETR) issues its HIP allocation to every housing authority, which consists of an annual capital guideline (ACG) and an allocation of specified capital grants (SCG). The SCG refers to expenditure on private sector renovation through the improvement grant system, and the ACG is broadly the amount available to be spent on the public sector stock. There are two further items to consider. When setting borrowing limits for each authority, the Department specifies the level of capital receipts taken into account (RTIA), which has the effect of reducing the permitted level of borrowing. However, supplementary credit approvals (SCAs), which increase the level of permitted borrowing, can be agreed by the Department for specific purposes. SCAs may be issued at any time.

They are usually given for estate regeneration schemes and other government initiatives.

The system introduced a fundamental change to the rules for the use of capital receipts. Only 25 per cent of receipts can be used for capital purposes. The remaining 75 per cent must be used to repay debt, despite the fact that councils face gigantic problems of repair and modernisation, and even though their housing debt is a tiny fraction of the current value of their property. There is about as much sense in this as there would be if a householder, faced with a leaking roof, were to use all his or her available cash to make a premature reduction in their outstanding mortgage.

Each council is issued with a single basic credit approval (BCA) for capital expenditure on all services in the coming year. This gives the council permission to meet capital expenditure by borrowing or credit arrangements. In fixing the BCA, the secretary of state can take account of the usable capital receipts belonging to that council. A council which is deemed to have a low need to spend and a high level of capital receipts can find itself with a BCA of zero. The BCA covers all council services, and there is no ring-fence around capital. Councils can, therefore, decide to use housing credit approvals and housing capital receipts for non-housing purposes, and vice versa. However, in practice there is a limit to the amount that can be borrowed for housing because the Department tells each authority the maximum level of loan charges eligible for the HRA subsidy each year. Borrowing approvals can only be used in the year to which they relate. Any unused allocation cannot be carried forward and any overspending will be deducted from the following year's BCA.

There is no limit on the amount of capital expenditure which can be covered directly from revenue but the freedom is more cosmetic than actual. Any use of it will affect rent levels since no support can be given from the general fund.

Under the previous system, grants made by housing authorities to private owners for renovation or improvement of their property were financed by borrowing. Councils received an annual government subsidy towards the cost of the loan charges on such borrowing. Under the 1990 Act system, subsidy is by a lump sum grant called a specified capital grant (SCG).

Leasing arrangements on property, plant, vehicles and other items, widely used by councils in recent years, were brought within the capital control system. They must be taken into account when a council's aggregate credit limit (ACL) is calculated. This broadly consists of outstanding debt plus the council's credit arrangements. A council has no power to borrow if it would cause the ACL to be exceeded. The extent of 'credit cover' deemed to be used when a credit arrangement is entered into is the cost in the first and subsequent years, discounted by a formula determined by the secretary of state.

Besides all the constraints listed above, any borrowing must be from British-based lenders, unless there is consent to do otherwise.

In 1998 the Government outlined proposals to modify the existing system, with effect from April 2000. These proposals are examined later in this chapter but first it is necessary to consider the revenue side.

The housing revenue system in England and Wales

Again a little background is appropriate. Given that the Conservatives had been in power for a decade, and they had had one bite at reform in 1980, why was further change necessary? A good deal of the answer is that the 1980 Act system had been crumbling for some years, and, like the capital side, it was no longer producing the sorts of outcomes that the Government wanted. In particular, the subsidy system, which had been designed to enable the government to put pressure on councils to raise rents, was not working. The system consisted of two separate subsidies: a general housing subsidy and rent rate subsidy. General housing subsidy was tailored to meet notional deficits on the HRA while rent rebate subsidy met virtually the whole cost of rebates (housing benefit) paid to council tenants. The system allowed the government to withdraw general housing subsidy in line with assumed changes in levels of deficit. Rent rate subsidy could not be withdrawn in the same way even in cases where HRAs were in substantial surplus.

Most councils had lost all entitlement to general housing subsidy, and therefore the government could no longer put pressure on rents by withdrawing more subsidy. Only 95 councils were still receiving general housing subsidy in 1987/88 although all councils received rent rebate subsidy which met almost the total cost of rent rebates. Some councils, which were not getting housing subsidy, were nevertheless giving substantial help to the HRA from the rates, in some cases well above the amounts assumed in the calculation of the rate support grant. Others, which were receiving housing subsidy, were producing surpluses which they transferred to their general rate funds. Some managed to balance their HRAs with rate fund contributions which were less than the assessments on which they were receiving rate support grant. In other words, from the Government's point of view, public expenditure was not necessarily going where it was most needed.

In addition, the financial arrangements had failed to cope with changing circumstances. Because councils borrow on a historic cost basis, the cost of borrowing is eroded by inflation. This applies to house purchasers too, or anyone else who borrows in inflationary times. As a

Table 2
Typical housing revenue account

Expenditure		£000
Net debit for loan charges, 'item 8 debit'		2,780
Revenue contributions to capital outlay		
Supervision and management		
– general	855	
– special	496	
		1,351
Repairs & maintenance		2,956
HRA rents and rebates		4,240
Provision for irrecoverable rent arrears		15
Transfer to general fund		0
Rents, rates, taxes payable on HRA property		112
Other		0
Sub total		11,454
Working balance at end of year		607
Total		12,061

Income		
Gross rents		
– dwellings		8,565
– other property		338
Net HRA subsidy		1,816
Net credit from interest & loan charges (item 8 credit)		215
Transfer from general fund		0
Other income		117
Sub total		11,051
Working balance at start of year		1,010
Total		12,061

result, there was a growing tendency towards bigger surpluses in HRAs. The Government concluded that, since the financing of new building by councils has been partly offset by surpluses on earlier, low-cost building, an end to new building by councils would lead to further surpluses.

It believed that these surpluses should not be available as a cushion for what it labelled bad practice and inefficiency. The Government's view was that while rents should be affordable to people in low-paid employment and therefore, may have to be set below market levels, they should be set by reference to two parameters – what people can pay and what the property is worth – rather than by reference to historic cost. It is important to understand that central to the 1989 Act system was a clear strategy for rents and subsidies: rents generally should rise in real terms, and there should be a reduction in general housing subsidies, with greater reliance placed on income-related assistance with housing costs (ie housing benefit) targeted on those in need. This strategy for the council sector was broadly consistent with parallel changes being introduced in the private rented and housing association sectors.

The revenue finance system introduced in the 1989 Act was clearly a development from the 1980 Act system; for example, it retained the method of calculating subsidy on the basis of the notional deficit on the HRA, irrespective of the actual state of the account. Subsidy is payable to bridge the gap between approved expenditure and assumed income. The main items of expenditure are actual debt charges and allowances for management and maintenance. On the income side the key items are guideline rents and actual rent rebates. Calculation of subsidy in relation to notional deficits left councils a degree of freedom to set their own rents. However, it also gave the government considerable leverage on council decision making: the amount of subsidy actually received reflects the government's decisions about rents and management and maintenance. If the government decides that rents are to rise much faster than expenditure on management and maintenance then the notional deficit will fall, and actual subsidy will fall too. In this way the government can exert considerable leverage on councils to raise rents. It is important to see that the assumptions about changes in rental income and management and maintenance allowances work together: the greater the gap between them the greater the leverage on rents.

However, the new system differed from the old one in certain crucial ways. First, the HRA now has just one source of subsidy, known as the HRA subsidy, replacing what had previously been three quite separate and distinct forms of assistance: general subsidy, rent rebate subsidy and rate fund contributions. The effect of this move was to greatly expand what counted as the deficit on the HRA, thus returning virtually all authorities to the position where they were vulnerable to pressure to raise rents from subsidy withdrawal. The HRA subsidy consists of two elements, the rent rebate element (which is always a positive amount) and the housing element (which can be a negative amount). Thus:

HRA subsidy = Rebate element + or − Housing element.

The rebate element is simply the aggregate cost of housing benefit paid to the council's own tenants, and therefore it is always a large positive amount. The housing element, however, can be a negative amount: this arises where the income from rents exceeds approved expenditure. Where the housing element is negative, it reduces the HRA subsidy entitlement below the aggregate cost of rent rebates. This has given rise to the argument that some of the cost of rebates to help the least well off tenants is being borne by other tenants, rather than by tax payers at large. This will be referred to again later.

Second, the HRA is ring-fenced, so that councils cannot keep rents low by drawing on their council tax income, but nor can they keep the council tax low by creaming off surpluses from the HRA.

Third, whereas under the old system the determinations for rent increases and management and maintenance (M&M) allowances were the same for all authorities, under the 1990 Act system each authority gets its own guideline rent and M&M allowance each year.

Rent increases

The approach to rent setting in the 1990 Act system is based on progress towards rents which, while having regard to what people can pay, are also related to what the property is worth. It is important to be clear that this is not the same as capital value rents, ie rents set at say four per cent of the capital value. The Government's approach is to say only that rent *increases* should reflect differences in capital values. This involves assessing the capital value of the housing stock of each council, using Right to Buy sale values (before discount). From this, the total value of all council housing in the country is derived. Each authority's stock is expressed as a proportion of the total national value. If a council owned housing stock worth one per cent of the total then it would be expected to raise one per cent of the total rent income.

Each year the government decides the overall national increase in the coming year. This figure is then divided amongst the various housing authorities according to their share of the total value. It is an odd way of doing things. The vast difference in house prices across the country meant that as the system was being devised it soon became clear that it was producing some strange and unacceptable results. For example, the formula suggested that rents in the London Borough of Hillingdon would need to increase by 65 per cent. But rents in Blackburn should be reduced by 51 per cent.

The Government was obviously not going to accept that rents should go down anywhere. A system of 'damping' was introduced to ensure that rents everywhere continued to rise, but that nowhere had guideline increases that were politically unacceptable. The way that the damping system works is that it is designed to produce a given aggregate national increase, so that if the maximum increase in any area is kept low then more must be raised from councils with the minimum increase. It also works the other way round: if the government opts for a large maximum then the minimum is lower. Table 3 lists the range of guideline increases since 1990/91, showing how in years such as 1990/91 when the maximum increase was high the minimum was much lower than in the following year, when the maximum was kept down.

Table 3
Guideline rent increases in England, 1990/91–1999/00

Guideline increases	1990/91	1991/92	1992/93	1993/94	1994/95
Minimum	£0.95	£1.38	£1.20	£1.50	£1.50
Maximum	£4.50	£2.50	£4.50	£3.00	£2.90
Average guideline rent	£23.06	£24.90	£27.31	£29.43	£31.63
Guideline increases	**1995/96**	**1996/9**	**1997/98**	**1998/99**	**1999/00**
Minimum	£1.82	£0.67	£0.48	£0.72	£0.89
Maximum	£2.82	£1.17	£0.98	£1.22	£1.64
Average guideline rent	£33.88	£34.63	£35.36	£36.35	£37.62

In the early 1990s the Government pursued a policy of driving up council rents faster than inflation. In four of the first five years of the new system the real increase in guideline rents in England (ie the increase over and above inflation) was five per cent. The £4.50 maximum in 1990/91 was a very large increase, since £2.95 had been the highest guideline figure in the preceding ten years. But the new financial regime also allowed authorities to increase rents even further. The London Borough of Redbridge, for instance, increased rents in April 1990 by £15.64 a week (a 44 per cent increase) instead of the guideline 95p, Canterbury £12.29, (guideline £1.92), a 54 per cent increase, Bournemouth £9.00, guideline £1.32, a 33 per cent increase.

Some authorities continued to raise rents much faster than required by their guideline amounts. In the first few years, rents generally tended to rise by more than the guidelines. By 1993/94 the average council rent in England was £32.87, or almost 12 per cent above the average guideline. Average rents rose 33 per cent in real terms in the first four years of the system.

Council rents have risen by more than the guideline amounts for two main reasons. First, authorities have chosen to raise rents in order to pay for levels of management and maintenance above the DETR allowances. Secondly, they have funded an increased proportion of capital expenditure from revenue. Another possibility is that some councils used very high rent increases as an incentive to tenants to vote for transfer to another landlord.

It is also important to note that rent increases have been greater in some regions than others because of the Government's policy of relating guideline increases to property values. This has meant that most authorities in the north have had the minimum guideline increase each year, amounting to only £6.53 in five years, compared with the cumulative figure of £16.40 for those authorities (mostly in the south) given the maximum guideline increase each year.

In 1995 the Government began to retreat from its established policy of substantial real increases each year. The White Paper of July 1995 referred to the intention to move, over a run of years, towards lower real increases, simply raising rents in line with inflation. In practice, it was decided to adopt a zero rate of real increase from April 1996, and penalties were subsequently introduced to prevent councils from breaching the new policy. These penalties took the form of limits on the payment of rent rebate subsidy, so that the subsidy paid to the council is calculated on the guideline rent increase rather than the actual increase; it should be noted, however, that the housing benefit of individual tenants is not affected. The main reasons for this striking change of direction were that the Government was increasingly concerned about the cost of housing benefit, and the impact of high rents on work incentives. In other words, the new policy should be seen as government recognition of its failure to reform housing benefit rather than conversion to a low rent policy for its own sake.

In 1997 the incoming Labour Government maintained tight control of council rent increases; however, in 1998 it announced that guideline rents would rise by one per cent in real terms in 1999 and by two per cent in each of the next two years.

Management and maintenance

As mentioned above, management and maintenance allowances are crucial to the way the system works. Each council has separate allowances for management and for maintenance. They also have target figures for both management and maintenance. The Government's strategy has been to move towards the position where actual allowances were the same as targets. Where an authority has actual expenditure well below its target, it is encouraged to spend more by being given a higher allowance, while councils spending above their targets have been given little or no increase in actual allowance, and in some cases actual reductions have been imposed.

The Government makes assumptions about management and maintenance expenditure in each local authority area. In the first year, 1990/91, they merely rolled forward the old system and gave authorities an eight per cent increase. Since 1991/92, however, M&M allowances have been based on information about the characteristics of the stock in each area. This is not to say that allowances are based on a view of what particular authorities need to spend on their housing; instead the information on the stock is used as a way of dividing up the total amount that the Treasury has agreed should be available for M&M allowances. The idea is to target larger increases in allowances on those authorities deemed to be underspending according to the formula.

In 1991/92 the total increase was six per cent, but with inflation also assumed to be six per cent there was no increase in real terms. Authorities that were to be encouraged to spend more could only benefit from targeting if others received allowances increased by less than six per cent. In that year 44 authorities benefited, at the expense of 36 high spending authorities whose allowances were frozen at their 1990/91 levels, and all the rest whose allowances increased by a little less than inflation.

The following year the total allowance was increased by 6.5 per cent in cash, which was seen as two per cent in real terms. This time all authorities in England received at least 3.5 per cent extra in cash, while 135 benefited from targeting. In 1993/94 when there was a real increase of one per cent in the total amount, more than 57 per cent of English authorities received a nil cash increase in order to pay for targeting. In 1994/95 the total allowance was increased by four per cent (1.5 per cent in real terms), and again many authorities received nil cash increases to pay for targeting. In 1995/96 the national M&M allowances were increased by 3.75 per cent, with all the increase being channelled towards low spending councils. In 1996/97 the Government froze in cash terms the national provision for M&M allowances, but within this there was some redistribution from high spending councils (which faced actual cash decreases in their allowances) towards low spenders. The policy of freezing allowances in cash terms was continued in subsequent years.

Many councils have criticised the Government for the low levels of increase in M&M allowances, partly because of the lack of scope for service improvements and partly because of the effect of new restrictions on capital expenditure brought in under the 1989 Act. The previously widespread practice of borrowing or using capital receipts to meet the cost of major repairs was seriously restricted under the new capital system. The choice for many councils is therefore to cut repairs programmes, or further increase rents. Overall, councils have opted to spend considerably more on M&M than the allowances allocated by the Government.

The impact of the 1989 Act system

The 1989 Act meant a massive transfer of power to central government of virtually all meaningful decisions about council housing – on rent levels, on expenditure on maintenance, improvement and rehabilitation, and on management. Rents have risen substantially in real terms, and as a proportion of average wages, at a time when increasing proportions of council tenants have no work and rely on benefits for their entire income. Upwards pressure on rents was achieved by combining rent rebate subsidy with general housing subsidy, thereby ensuring that nearly every housing authority was entitled to HRA subsidy. It is the existence of subsidy which gives the government leverage on rents – without subsidy there is nothing to take away, and therefore no way of exerting pressure on councils to raise rents. However, by 1994/95 in three quarters of housing authorities in England the general subsidy element of HRA subsidy had become negative, and since then the proportion has continued to rise. This means that the HRA subsidy received is composed entirely of the rent rebate element, and that the negative housing element is subtracted from the rebate element, as explained earlier (see p28).

There are two important points to note here. First, council housing in England and Wales as a whole is no longer in receipt of general housing subsidy, a situation that had never existed until the 1990s. Second, the overall net surplus (gross surplus minus the cost of housing subsidy for authorities remaining in deficit) has risen year by year. It reached £710 million in England by 1998/99, providing a substantial contribution (30 per cent) towards the cost of rent rebates paid to council tenants. This has led some people to argue that tenants who pay the full rent are in effect contributing towards the cost of the housing benefit claimed by their less well off neighbours. There is certainly some force in this argument, especially when it is remembered that other landlords, housing associations and private owners, do not have their surpluses creamed off in the same way. However, it is important to acknowledge that no council tenant ever faces a rent rise simply in order to enable someone else to receive a rent rebate.

Over the years, since the introduction of the 1989 Act, gross HRA surpluses have amounted to nearly £7 billion. Much of this has been reclaimed from local authorities by the Government, money which critics of the system say should have been available to the local authorities to use to improve services or to reduce rents. The problem with this position is that it is difficult to persuade the Treasury that taxpayers as a whole should subsidise HRAs that are in surplus. Moreover, council HRAs generate surpluses on rents that are, on average, well below those charged by housing associations and private landlords.

An important factor in the generation of surpluses is the relationship between rents and management and maintenance expenditure. It is necessary to remember that the gross surplus of £1.3 billion in 1998/99 is the *notional* surplus on the national HRA, and that the key variables that affect the size of this surplus are the guideline rents and management and maintenance allowances set by government, not the actual rents or actual expenditure on M&M. Changes to the assumptions fed into the subsidy calculation could very quickly affect the number of authorities running notional surpluses. In the early 1990s, when the Government's priority was to force up council rents in real terms, the mechanism for putting pressure on councils to make increases was withdrawal of subsidy. By using rising rental income to fund subsidy reductions rather than increased expenditure on M&M the government was the agent of disrepair. This leads to the conclusion that rather than focusing on rents and surpluses we should be looking at the low levels of M&M allowances and asking why councils are not allowed to spend more on improving their houses.

A new approach: resource accounting

Towards the end of 1998 the Government issued a consultation paper (*A New Financial Framework for Local Authority Housing: Resource Accounting in the Housing Revenue Account*), which was a follow-up to the publication of the comprehensive spending review in the summer. Resource accounting sounds dry and uninteresting; it is also a term which conveys little of its significance, but it represents a fundamental change in the method of accounting for local authority housing. It means a departure from the methods and principles used since subsidies were introduced 80 years ago. The Government's view is that the current system does not encourage efficient investment; the new approach will, apparently, be more business-like and more transparent. We shall see.

The key change is the abandonment of a perfectly transparent system in which the debt charges falling on the HRA are directly related to the actual borrowing historically incurred in order to create the assets. Resource accounting involves a move away from historic costs to current values. The consultation paper describes it as a method of measuring on a consistent basis the resources used over the lifetime of houses, rather than simply the cash spent on them each year. The argument is that historic debt charges do not reflect the true costs of the capital tied up in housing assets, nor the true level of subsidy. Under resource accounting, each local authority will have to produce a figure for the current value of its housing stock. Each year the expenditure side of the HRA will have to show an amount equal to six per cent of the valuation. In other words, councils will be expected to generate a rate of return of six per cent on their housing assets. It is essential to note that the introduction of the six per cent annual charge for

capital does not mean that councils have to charge rents on individual houses at levels that would generate this rate of return.

In future, instead of showing the actual expenditure on interest and debt repayment, the HRA will contain a capital charge consisting of two elements, the cost of capital and an allowance for depreciation or major repairs. The cost of capital is the six per cent figure mentioned above, and in most authorities it is expected to exceed the actual expenditure on debt servicing. The full cost of capital is to be paid into a separate account (Asset Management Revenue Account), from which will be paid sums necessary to meet actual debt charges, with the surplus being paid to the DETR.

At the time of writing the consultation paper the DETR had not finally decided whether to opt for an allowance for depreciation or major repairs, but the intention was that some kind of allowance would be paid as part of the subsidy calculation. It is expected that over time the allowance would become the main source of funding for major repairs, thereby reducing the need for further borrowing.

Another key issue left unresolved in the consultation paper is the basis of calculating the value of the stock. It comes down to a choice between 'open market value' and 'existing use value (social housing)'. The latter is the basis of valuation used for stock transfers to other landlords, and in the registered social landlord (RSL) sector. It seems the most sensible one to use in this context, given the Government's stated aim of achieving comparability between local authorities and RSLs. Whatever basis is adopted, there will need to be an initial stock valuation exercise, followed at intervals by some sort of revaluation.

Under the 1989 Act, expenditure on rent rebates is charged to the HRA and funded (in full or in part) by subsidy on the income side of the account, as discussed above. The consultation paper proposes to end this controversial arrangement. Instead, it proposes to charge the cost of rebates to the authority's general fund (ie the account dealing with income and expenditure for non-housing services), with appropriate Exchequer subsidy. However, critics of the current system can draw no comfort from this because in a revealing passage the consultation paper says:

'... the Government would still need to 'capture' surplus rental income to offset the additional costs of funding rent rebates in full. The Government does not intend that the change to funding rent rebates from the non-HRA General fund should increase the aggregate of capital and revenue spending on repairs to council housing. The Government would therefore need to make alternative arrangements to capture and redistribute the notional rental surpluses, or other provision of equal value.'

Just how this will be done is a matter for further consultation.

On the all important question of rents, resource accounting is presented as having only very limited impact, at least in the short term. Rents will still be set by councils at below market levels. Existing arrangements for guideline rents will continue, along with incentives to encourage councils not to increase rents above guideline levels. However, the consultation paper notes that councils already have an obligation to have regard to the general pattern of private sector rents in their area when setting their own rents. It also comments that most councils do not vary their rents enough to fully reflect differences in size, location and other characteristics. In the longer

Table 4
Housing revenue operating account

Expenditure	£m
Management & maintenance	9.600
Cost of capital*	9.000
Major repairs contribution	
to Housing Repairs Account	2.000
Other debits	1.200
Sub total	21.800

Income	
Actual rent	14.100
Other income	1.000
Housing subsidy	6.000
Other credits	1.200
Sub total	22.300

Net cost of services	0.500
Capital expenditure	
financed from revenue	0.000
Surplus for the year	0.500

* Note to HRA cost of capital calculation:

Housing stock value £150m @ 6 per cent = £9m (of this £3m is notional interest paid to the Asset Management Revenue Act (AMRA), £1m is Minimum Revenue Provision, ie contribution towards repayment of debt principal, and £5m is paid to the DETR.)

This is based on the DETR consultation paper, *A New Financial Framework for Local Authority Housing : Resource Accounting in the Housing Revenue Account*, December 1998.

run it is possible that the Government will move towards insisting that individual rents reflect capital values.

The Government's own assessment of the longer term impact of resource accounting is that it will result in a shift from capital to revenue funding for major repairs (with a corresponding decrease in annual credit approvals). The Government also believes that it 'should assist authorities to consider moving to a more arms-length management of council housing' (ie stock transfer).

The sale of council houses

Almost from the start of large-scale council housing in 1919 some authorities sold small numbers of houses to better off tenants. Councils enjoyed the right to sell, more or less continuously, up to 1980. Some councils were more enthusiastic than others, and the discounts offered varied from place to place, but the overall rate of sales remained very low, especially when compared with rates of new building. It was during the 1970s that Conservative controlled Birmingham City Council demonstrated that high levels of sales could be achieved. This was picked up by the Conservative Party nationally and turned into a major campaigning issue at the general election of May 1979. Instead of councils having a discretionary right to sell, the Tories promised to introduce a statutory right for tenants to buy their homes, even in situations where the council was reluctant to sell. Accordingly the Housing Act, 1980, gave council tenants the right to buy their homes at substantial discounts and began the process of transforming public housing in Britain.

The Right to Buy applies to any tenant of two years or more, except for those in dwellings designed or specially adapted for old people. After two years tenants have the right to purchase at market value less a discount of 32 per cent, with a further one per cent for every extra year's tenancy up to a maximum of 60 per cent. The discount on flats starts at 40 per cent, and increases at the rate of two per cent a year, reaching a maximum of 70 per cent after 15 years.

There are two situations in which tenants, who would qualify for the full discount, are not entitled to it. The first arises where the discount would reduce the sale price below the so-called 'cost floor'. Where an authority has incurred expenditure on building, acquiring or improving a house in the previous ten years (including repair and maintenance expenditure in excess of £5,500), the discount cannot reduce the purchase price below the total of these costs. Thus, for example, in the case of a house valued at £50,000 and occupied by a tenant entitled to a 60 per cent discount of £30,000, the normal selling price would be £20,000. If the council had carried out a major refurbishment costing £25,000 then the

minimum price would be set at £25,000. The second situation is where the percentage discount produces a cash figure above the permitted maximum. When the right to buy was introduced the maximum discount was £25,000, later increased to £50,000; in early 1999 a new set of regional maxima were introduced, reducing the maximum discounts to 70 per cent of the regional average market value of council houses (65 per cent in London), together with a national maximum of £38,000.

Before the introduction of the Right to Buy councils had provided a very useful house purchase finance service which supplemented the facilities given by other lenders. Councils had the freedom to fix the terms so long as they did not involve the ratepayers in a loss. They usually charged interest at a quarter or a half per cent above their average loans pool rate which applied to other council borrowing. The 1980 Act changed this by requiring councils to charge the recommended building societies rate, or its own average loans pool rate plus a quarter per cent, whichever was the higher. So when society rates were below the council's pool rate plus 0.25 per cent, the society rates did not apply. When society rates were higher, councils had to charge building society rates, though there was no need for it – the worst of both worlds.

Not surprisingly, most council house sales were financed by the building societies and banks. Suddenly, with the steep rise in interest rates in 1989, councils found themselves charging 14.5 per cent on their mortgage loans, about 3-4 per cent more than is needed – average loans pool rates are mostly between ten and eleven per cent. The damage and hardship which the system inflicts on those who chose a council mortgage, usually the less well off purchasers, are manifest.

Financial effects of sales

The sale of council housing stock resulted in savings on the council's repair bills and perhaps some saving on management costs. Against this, it lost the rent and any housing subsidy payable.

Sales financed by a council mortgage loan provide the council with regular repayments on the outstanding loan but no lump sum capital receipts. Most sales, however, are financed from banks and building societies in which case the council receives the whole of the sale price at once. There is the added advantage that capital receipts are not credited to the housing revenue account. They are used to reduce the council's housing debt, or added to other housing capital receipts and used for capital spending, or invested.

If the proceeds are invested, there will be investment income, and this goes to the income side of the housing revenue account. Since April 1990, 75 per cent of capital receipts has to be allocated to the redemption of debt charges, thereby reducing costs falling on the HRA. Receipts used for new capital expenditure benefit the HRA by reducing borrowing and thus debt charges.

There is no doubt about the advantages of the Right to Buy scheme for the majority of those who can afford to buy. For the council, however, the advantages of sales are a matter of some controversy. The selling price, even after the huge discount, will generally be much more than the outstanding debt on the house. It has therefore been argued that selling cannot fail to be profitable. This is like saying that someone who sells a house worth £50,000 which was bought long ago for £10,000 and with an outstanding mortgage loan of say £6,000, gains £14,000 by selling for £20,000. This is obvious nonsense. An asset worth £50,000 has been exchanged for £20,000 cash. The net proceeds are £14,000 when they ought to be £44,000.

There are two even more important issues. First, there is the elementary question as to what sense there can be in selling houses so far below their real value that it will take several sales to provide one replacement of similar quality; and this at a time of scarcity of rented accommodation. Second, the alleged profitability of such sales is an illusion. The immediate apparent gain – investment income on sale proceeds which exceeds rent income – is real enough the first year, but is less the year after by the amount by which the rent would have risen if the house had been retained. In a few years a crossover point is reached and the gains turn into losses of ever greater magnitude.

A financial appraisal of the effects of sales was in fact produced for the Labour government in 1977, but not published. It showed sales as resulting in profits to councils in the earlier years, as mortgage repayments exceeded what the rents would have been, turning into substantial losses in later years as rents continued to increase. A second paper, done for the new Conservative government in 1980 (presumably by the same civil servants, with admirable flexibility of mind) showed continuing profits. The different answer resulted from the different assumptions made in the second paper about future subsidies, costs, and rent increases.

A study, carried out for the House of Commons Environment Select Committee and published in 1981, found that some of the assumptions which enabled the second paper to portray sales as yielding a profit were totally unrealistic. It calculated that, in fact, the long-term losses on council house sales, calculated over a 50 year period, were likely to average £12,500 per dwelling. Yet even these calculations did not allow for the enormous rent increases which have actually occurred since 1981.

Another sleight of hand by the DETR was its claim that it would generously allow councils to supplement their HIP allocations with capital receipts from sales. This would increase the amount they could spend on housing provision or improvement. At first the DETR said 50 per cent, then 40 per cent, then 20 per cent.

Restrictions on the use of capital receipts in the 1980s resulted in a huge accumulation of receipts in local authority coffers, reaching £6 billion in the late 1980s. Meanwhile authorities saw their HIP allocations reduced year after year as the condition of their housing stocks declined. The money was there to tackle the problems of disrepair and modernisation, but the Government made it even more difficult to spend. The Local Government and Housing Act, 1989 required authorities to use receipts to write off old debts rather than invest in better housing, as discussed above.

Moving on from the strictly financial effects of council house sales, there are one or two further points to be made, about the impact of sales on council housing as a whole. Over the period since 1980 1.7 million council houses and flats have been sold under the Right to Buy (plus other dwellings sold under different arrangements). This has meant that the total supply of council homes has fallen by 30 per cent. Sales have not been evenly distributed across the country or the stock. Research by Colin Jones and Alan Murie (*Reviewing the Right to Buy*, 1998) has shown that levels of sales have tended to be higher in areas where home-ownership rates were already high, such as the south east, and lower in areas with lower rates of home-ownership, such as the north of England. Some authorities have sold more than 40 per cent of their housing stock through the Right to Buy, while other have sold less than 20 per cent. Sales have also tended to be concentrated on the most attractive and desirable estates, and among houses with gardens rather than flats, despite the very high discounts available. The sorts of people who have been attracted by the opportunity to buy have been the better off tenants in secure and reasonably well paid jobs. They have been people in the middle stages of the life cycle, so that council housing has become more obviously a tenure occupied by elderly and very young tenants. The Right to Buy has changed the social composition of council housing, increasing the proportion of tenants on very low incomes, and reducing the proportion who have an earned income.

Large scale voluntary transfers

In the period since 1988, the transfer of the entire stock of council dwellings in a local authority area has become a well-established aspect of current policy. Therefore it is important to remember just how revolutionary a proposal it was when first discussed. The trigger was the so-called 'tenants' choice' provisions of the Housing Act, 1988. Under tenants' choice private landlords were given the right to bid for selected parts of the council stock, subject to a ballot of tenants. The prospect of profit-seeking private landlords taking over entire stocks of council housing (or picking off the best estates) raised fears about the possible long-term loss of social rented housing available on the basis of need at affordable rents. Some councils started to take the initiative and to plan to transfer their own housing to new housing associations set up for the purpose. Such associations, run by boards made up of a mix of tenants, councillors and others, would be able to preserve the values of social housing. They would have better access than local authorities to capital for improving the quality and quantity of affordable rented housing. This was because the Treasury was committed to public expenditure conventions which prevent local authorities themselves from borrowing the capital they need to improve their houses. Thus large scale voluntary transfer (LSVT) developed not as an aspect of government policy but as a way of getting round it. Subsequently, of course, the Government seized upon LSVT as a good idea and put councils under increasing pressure to go down this route.

The first successful transfer was achieved in December 1988, when Chiltern District Council, in Buckinghamshire, transferred its stock to Chiltern Hundreds Housing Association. By the end of March 1999, eighty eight councils, mostly in southern England, had transferred 352,000 dwellings to new landlords – in nearly every case, a specially created housing association. The transfer programme was cranked up by the Conservatives in the mid-1990s, and the pace has hardly slackened under the Labour Government. Indeed the programme for 1999-2000, announced in March 1999, covers 140,000 dwellings in 19 English local authorities. For the first time a number of very large proposals from large cities, such as Coventry, with 20,000 dwellings, are being considered. For some years the Scots and Welsh stood back from transfers, but by 1998 some of the largest Scottish cities were committed to the principle. In early 1999 the Government announced plans that might lead to a quarter of Scottish council houses being transferred within three years.

In financial terms LSVT is essentially a remortgaging exercise, much like a home-owner with a small mortgage in relation to the value of their property, who raises cash for improvements by taking out a new loan. In the case of council housing this process requires a transfer of ownership but the principle is the same. LSVT is a way of breaking out of the public expenditure conventions which have led to such severe limitations on local authority freedom to invest. One of the great advantages of LSVT is that the new associations are not counted as part of the public sector. So they are free to borrow as much as their rental income will permit. In the case of the councils that transferred in the first decade of LSVT, the value of the stock was greater (sometimes much greater) than the outstanding debt. Therefore the council recouped a significant capital receipt. Now, however, ways are being actively sought to enable the larger urban authorities to benefit from transfer, even though their stock may have a very low value compared with the debt.

The financial basis of LSVT is that the stock is sold at much less than would be obtained by selling the houses individually under the Right to Buy; the average price per dwelling in the period 1988-1998 was less than £9,500 (the lowest unit price was just £2,525 in Walsall and the highest was £13,750 in West Somerset). These prices reflect the fact that the dwellings are not offered with vacant possession but with sitting tenants (who have security of tenure and certain retained rights, such as the right to buy). Valuations also take into account the need to spend on repairs and improvement, and the fact that there are restrictions on the rate at which rental income can be increased.

From the point of view of the local authority, a key to the financial success of LSVT was the fact that housing associations, unlike councils, are not required to use surplus rental income to subsidise the cost of housing benefit (see above); in other words, there is a continuing revenue cost borne by the Treasury, and in 1993/94 the Government introduced a levy of 20 per cent of capital receipts arising from LSVT (net of outstanding debt) as a way of recouping some of this cost. However, in order to promote transfers the Budget of 1996 suspended the levy for three years.

As mentioned above, LSVT was introduced as a reaction to government policy but it has now become a mainstream policy in its own right. It looks set to be increasingly important in future, driven forward by financial advantages. In one sense, it is completely unnecessary because, of course, the distinction between borrowing by a local authority (bad) and a housing association (good) is entirely artificial. The money still has to be raised, possibly from the same lenders, and it is spent on exactly the same houses. The only difference is that council borrowing counts as public expenditure, which must be controlled, and borrowing by housing associations does not count as public expenditure and is therefore unregulated.

Finally, financial reasons are a pretext for transfer in LSVT. Removing housing from direct provision by local authorities is consistent with wider moves to fragment and diversify the provision of public services, properly provided by and subject to the control of democratically elected local councils.

The costs of homelessness

It is impossible to be precise about the costs of homelessness. How can a monetary value be placed on broken relationships, ruined childhoods and lost job opportunities? One thing we can be certain of is that the cost of homelessness in this wider sense is far greater than the financial expenditure involved. In terms of public expenditure, in a sense all the money spent by councils and most of that spent by housing associations on the provision of homes is about the prevention or relief of homelessness.

However, funds specifically earmarked for the relief of homelessness amount to only a very minor part of the total volume of housing public expenditure. In 1989 the Government announced a package of measures costing £250 million over two years. Conditions attached to the deal made it clear that councils had to channel resources into housing association provision and that they themselves were not going to be able to build new houses.

This package followed a period during which homelessness had been increasing rapidly and the Government had appeared to be uninterested in the problem. The 1987 White Paper on housing failed to mention homelessness. Yet between 1978 and 1992 there was a 180 per cent increase in the numbers of homeless households accepted by local authorities in England. The Government eventually decided to introduce legislation to amend the rights of homeless people but, instead of strengthening their rights, the Housing Act, 1996 reduced them significantly by taking away the right to permanent accommodation. The Labour Party fought the 1997 general

Figure 1

Numbers of households accepted as homeless, and numbers of homeless households in temporary accommodation, 1990-97 (GB)

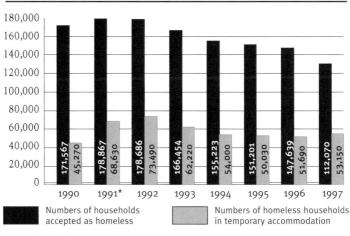

Source: Wilcox S., *Housing Finance Review 1998-99* (1998)

Source: *Information Bulletin Homelessness Statistics* DETR (1999)

*in 1991 the way of compiling figures was changed and the new category of 'homeless at home' was introduced

election on a promise of restoring the rights of homeless people, but so far there has been no sign of new legislation.

By 1990 the Government's concern had grown to the extent of two further measures to try to reduce the visible presence of homeless people on the streets. The first was an increase in the support given to voluntary housing aid and advice agencies and the second was the announcement of a package designed to get single homeless people off the streets of London.

The Rough Sleepers Initiative began with a budget of £96 million over three years. This was subsequently extended and the programme was expanded to take in cities such as Bristol which were seen to have high levels of street homelessness. Under the third phase of the Initiative, 1996-97 to 1998-99, £73 million was made available to continue the work. A separate budget of £16 million was available in Scotland for 1997-98 to 1999-2000.

In 1998 the Labour Government announced changes to the established policy, including a commitment to reducing the numbers of people sleeping rough by two-thirds by 2002. In relation to London a new programme of £145 million was launched, with a further £34 million for the rest of England, and £14 million for Scotland. Moving on from the RSI the new Government has re-packaged its policy as the Homeless Action Programme, involving more than 250 national and local schemes.

These Government initiatives are on top of the action taken by local authorities in discharge of their statutory obligations to homeless people. In 1997-98 councils in England and Wales spent more than £155 million on homelessness, of which nearly 60 per cent was spent in London. Some £57 million was spent on providing bed and breakfast accommodation, at a gross cost of £12,500 per household per year – considerably more than the first year costs of providing a new council house. Bed and breakfast accommodation is both expensive for local authorities and highly unsatisfactory for families but its use continues – and some people have to put up with it for two years or more. Figures published in March 1999, suggest that use of bed and breakfast hotels is rising again, topping 14,500 for the first time since 1993.

3   Housing Associations

At the end of the twentieth century housing associations are the fastest growing and most dynamic part of the British housing system. Formally, housing associations are independent, private organisations providing housing and care services for low income households on a not-for-profit basis. They are run by boards of unpaid directors, but staffed by salaried professionals. Housing associations are by far the largest group of registered social landlords (RSLs), although there are now growing numbers of local housing companies and trusts that are also RSLs. Altogether there are more than 2,400 RSLs in Great Britain. Most of their stock is concentrated in England, where 90 per cent is owned by the 215 associations with more than 1,000 dwellings each, and a quarter of the stock belongs to the 15 associations with more than 10,000 dwellings each.

Long before councils became involved in the provision of rented housing, voluntary housing organisations, the forerunners of modern housing associations, sought to provide decent accommodation at affordable rents. There were two main types, the model dwellings companies, which sought to raise capital from people willing to lend below the normal rate of interest, and charitable trusts, established by wealthy benefactors. The model dwellings companies have disappeared, but some charitable trusts (notably the Peabody, Guinness and William Sutton Trusts, which are among the largest associations operating today) have survived and made the transition into modern housing associations.

In the nineteenth century almost all the voluntary sector housing activity was concentrated in London. Later the movement spread and, after the First World War, government subsidies became available on the same basis as those paid to local authorities. Despite this, the voluntary organisations struggled to raise enough capital to make an impact. Later, new kinds of organisations such as cost-rent, co-ownership, co-operative and self-build were tried; by far the major provision was still of dwellings for rent for those in need. However, the total stock, less than 250,000 dwellings by 1970, was still tiny and insignificant compared to the five million or so then provided by councils.

The 1970-74 Conservative Government decided upon a great expansion of the housing association movement as a supplement (or perhaps as an alternative) to council housing. The Housing Corporation, set up in 1964 to encourage the formation of cost-rent and co-ownership societies, was chosen to encourage the formation of housing associations to provide accommodation at fair rents. The Corporation would have an important supervisory function: it would examine and approve schemes, and the Government would provide the necessary financial support.

A Bill to provide the relevant powers was drafted but, before it reached the statute book, the 1974 Labour Government came into office. It promptly took over the previous Government's measure without alteration. With the Housing Act 1974, the great expansion began.

Shelter had played a notable part in the growth of the movement. It raised some £3 million by national appeals in 1969 and 1970, which it used mainly to start housing associations in areas of severe housing stress, and so supplement the work of the local authorities. By 1971, the associations were providing an extra 10,000 dwellings a year, a big increase on anything they had managed previously. With the impetus provided by the financial arrangements of the 1974 Act and the work of the Housing Corporation, this more than trebled by 1976, with 35,300 completions. In 1979 the election of a Conservative Government bent on cutting public expenditure and promoting home-ownership meant that housing associations were marginalised again for a number of years. They produced fewer new and converted dwellings than in the late 1970s. Annual completions during the first half of the 1980s never exceeded 16,600, and by 1986 had fallen to 12,571.

The associations have widened the choice open to would-be tenants. This has been especially important because some associations have displayed a willingness to house groups who have, in the past, been excluded from council accommodation. In more recent times, however, they have been required to give priority to homeless households and generally to shoulder a greater proportion of the task of housing the least well off.

Finance for the post-1974 expansion

The dramatic progress from 1974 onwards resulted from a new subsidy system, although the word 'subsidy' was tactfully avoided. From then on it was 'capital grants' or housing association grant (HAG). Previously, when subsidies were given, as in the local authority sector, they had been annual contributions to revenue outlay to meet part of the running costs. Now they were once-for-all lump sum grants which met most of the capital cost immediately. With these went a new rent system, 'fair rents', set by rent officers, as in the private sector.

The starting point for the new system was the rent which the rent officer recommended. The likely annual costs of management and maintenance, which would be the first call on the rent income, were then estimated. What was left after meeting those costs would be available for meeting loan charges on any money borrowed. It would not be very much and would service a loan which would meet only a small proportion of the total capital cost of providing the dwellings. The rest, the major part of the capital cost, was met by an outright capital grant (HAG). The system later came to be known as 100 per cent public funded which meant that, in addition to the grant, the loan element was provided by the Housing Corporation.

It was remarkably generous compared with previous systems with grant covering 80 per cent or more of approved capital costs (and grant at this sort of level, or even more, continued to be available until 1989). The associations were scarcely able to believe their good fortune. But this special treatment was needed for associations to expand. Unlike local councils, they did not have large stocks of earlier built low-cost housing to enable them to keep the rents of new houses affordable through rent pooling. The 1974 Act system of HAG and fair rents meant that associations operated in a virtually risk-free environment. If the Housing Corporation approved a scheme for grant aid then they could afford to build it, and pay for it in the long run. The Housing Corporation even provided short-term loans to enable associations to meet costs incurred during the development process, before the long-term loan was settled and before rental income began to come in. There could also be a second subsidy, a 'revenue deficit grant'. Because of controls on rents, associations could find themselves in deficit on the revenue account. A case could then be made to the DETR for grant assistance on the year's operations. The grant would not be a continuing one unless the need could be shown to persist.

The system placed associations in a luxurious position which could not last forever, and the surprising thing is that it continued as long as it did. The enthusiasm of many councils for the new scheme was limited. They compared it with their own subsidy scheme but they welcomed the greater variety and freedom of choice for tenants. The enthusiasm of the Treasury was likewise restrained, for the immediate cost was very heavy.

There was one astonishing oversight in the 1974 Act and this concerned the impact of inflation over time. Inflation causes rents to rise. A capital grant (HAG) which was appropriate when the grant was given would be too generous a few years later when the rents had gone up substantially after several rent reviews. A scheme which broke even at first, would soon be making a surplus. Yet the subsidy had all been given in one lump sum. It could not, like an annual subsidy, be reduced in future years when the need was less.

The light eventually dawned on the DETR, and the Housing Act 1980 required associations to keep a 'grant redemption fund' (GRF) into which surpluses on HAG-aided schemes were paid. Thus, the DETR could get part of its money back, or require surpluses to be used, for instance, for major repairs which otherwise would require grant aid.

Rents before the 1988 Act

The fair rents which housing associations charged as a condition of receiving HAG were generally higher than for comparable council dwellings. The difference narrowed as the 1980 Act produced drastic rent increases for council housing but widened again as council rent increases slowed down. As housing subsidies were reduced year after year until they ceased altogether for most councils outside London, the DETR lost much of its leverage for forcing rent increases on unwilling councils. In the meantime, fair rents were continuing their uninterrupted upward course.

The Housing Act 1988

Since 1988 housing associations have assumed a much more central position in housing policy, taking over from the local authorities as the main providers of new affordable rented housing. To expand their output without a corresponding increase in public expenditure, the Government radically changed the financial framework within which associations operate. The strategy involved changes to both the capital and revenue sides of housing association finances.

On the capital side the grant system remained in place, initially with no significant changes in the rate of the grant. However, the grant was now to be calculated before a scheme was built rather than after, which exposed associations to the risk of rising costs – an important change. Associations were encouraged to raise the non-grant aided part of their capital costs from private lending institutions (banks and building societies).
The introduction of private finance was of major importance for it exposed associations to greater risk. It also meant that a given amount of public expenditure could be spread across the production of more dwellings. Private finance also implied higher rents, if only because the lenders would require higher interest on loans than the government had previously charged.

On the revenue side, all new lettings created since 15 January 1989 have been assured tenancies. The fair rent system is being phased out and associations themselves have responsibility for setting rents on a growing proportion of their stock. The Government wanted rents to rise in real terms while remaining within the bounds of affordability. Low income tenants were to be compensated for higher rents by housing benefit in what was a conscious shift from general subsidy to income related assistance.

The 1988 Act also set up separate bodies to oversee the funding and regulation of associations: the Housing Corporation retained responsibility for England, while in Scotland it was replaced by Scottish Homes, and in Wales by Tai Cymru (Housing for Wales). Since 1 January 1999, the latter has been absorbed within the Welsh Office.

The Housing Act, 1996, made a number of changes to the powers of the Housing Corporation, including the power to give grant aid to organisations that were not housing associations (hence the introduction of the wider term Registered Social Landlords). At the same time the label HAG was dropped and replaced by social housing grant (SHG).

How the system works

The system works on the basis of an annual cycle of bids and allocations. Each autumn the associations wishing to build new houses and/or to acquire and rehabilitate old ones, put forward schemes to be funded by SHG. In the new year the Housing Corporation announces the allocations of grant to successful associations. The total amount to be distributed is set by the government in the Approved Development Programme (ADP). The Corporation divides the funds according to identified needs and priorities. It is rare for the Corporation to award a grant to a scheme that has not been prioritised within a local authority's local housing strategy. Local authorities can also contribute from their own resources (in the form of free or discounted land, or capital subsidy, known as local authority SHG). Local contributions can be a valuable way of enhancing funds available from the Corporation, and tweaking investment to reflect local priorities.

Through its control of the purse strings the government, via the Corporation, is in a strong position to steer associations towards certain types of work and particular categories of need. The quantity of new housing provided, the type of tenure offered (rented or shared ownership) and the people likely to benefit all reflect government priorities. The volume of grant aid available within the ADP is a key factor in determining the total number of dwellings provided, but so too is the rate of grant per dwelling. Both have been subject to change over the years since the current system began. In the first few years the emphasis was on increasing inputs into the ADP, which grew by a factor of three between 1988/89 and 1992/93. Thereafter, the ADP went into a steep decline for several years, to little more than a quarter of the 1992/93 level in 1998/99. Output was maintained by reductions in the level of subsidy per dwelling, and by a policy of encouraging associations to bid for grants at less than the official headline rate.

The overall average level of grant fell fast from 75 per cent in the early years to 62 per cent in 1994/95, and then in further stages to 54 per cent by 1998/99. It is important to note that these are average figures, which mask wide regional variations related to costs. Reductions in grant rate implied increases in private finance, with corresponding increases in rents. At first it was unclear to anyone whether the lenders would be prepared to invest sufficient capital in housing associations, given their non-profit making philosophy. However, associations worked very hard to make themselves attractive to lenders. The flow of funds was initially rather slow, but over the years they have raised huge amounts of private finance on satisfactory terms. The total amount raised in the decade ending in 1998, including funding for LSVTs, was nearly £14 billion, or around 40 per cent of the capital base of the sector.

One reason for the very large capital programme in 1992/93 was the housing market package (HMP), which was launched by the chancellor in November 1992. This was a desperate attempt by the Government to mop up unsold privately owned houses and thereby to put some life back into the deeply depressed housing market. Selected associations (81 in all) were given just 93 working days to spend £577 million (plus £328 million of private finance), but they managed it, and bought more than 18,000 houses. The injection of public expenditure in the HMP was not additional money but represented funds brought forward from future years. The effect, therefore, was to give associations a hectic time during the winter of 1992/93. It left them with less money to spend on the conventional, planned programme in the following period.

'Affordable' rents

Affordability has been one of the big issues for housing associations in the 1990s. Until 1989 they did not have to worry about rent levels because these were set externally by the independent rent officer service. However, now associations have to set their own rents on all new lettings (both new build and relets of existing stock). The government has required them to keep rents affordable for people in low paid work. At the same time the government has introduced measures (specifically the use of private finance and lower grant rates) which have put strong upward pressure on rents.

For tenants who were in their homes before the new system started in 1989, their tenancies continue to be secure with fair rents set by the rent officer. Fair rents are reviewed every two years.

For properties provided under the new regime, associations are expected to set rents which cover costs while still being affordable for tenants on low incomes. Affordability is the term used by the government but ministers and the Housing Corporation have steadfastly refused to give a clear definition (although Sir George Young, the Housing Minister in 1993 did let slip in evidence to the Select Committee on the Environment that the DETR takes 35 per cent of net income to be an affordable level of expenditure on rent). This is, of course, a problem for the associations and as a result there has been considerable debate about the best way to define affordability.

The National Housing Federation (NHF) has been very active on the issue of affordability. It has produced a regularly updated table of 'indicative rents' for all the ten sizes of dwelling and all the geographical areas for which the cost tables cater. Initially the NHF took 20 per cent as the affordable level, but it moved on to 22 per cent, and in 1993 adopted a new policy:

'Rents are affordable if the majority of working households taking up new tenancies are not caught in the poverty trap (because of dependency on housing benefit) or paying more than 25% of their net income on rent.' (Housing Associations Weekly, 21 January 1994)

In overall terms, rents have increased rapidly since 1988, at rates faster than prices and incomes. The gap between actual rents and the NHF affordability measure has widened year by year.

The rent surplus fund

There was, under the previous arrangements, the requirement to keep a grant redemption fund (GRF). Now each association must keep a rent surplus fund (RSF) which is different in important respects from the previous GRF.

The RSF arrangements do not apply to dwellings provided under the post-1988 regime. RSF rules apply only to old HAG schemes with their fair rents, where these are still charged, and the usually higher rents of houses re-let as assured tenancies. Gross rent income is calculated on the fair rents and, for re-lets, the higher of the actual rents is charged or the association's average fair rents. From this gross rent income is deducted a four per cent allowance for voids and bad debts; loan charges; management and maintenance expenditure; service charges; miscellaneous items; and rent losses which can arise when a new HAG dwelling is occupied by a tenant who retains security and fair rent rights.

From the net income thus calculated, the association must transfer 80 per cent to a sinking fund to meet the cost of future major repairs. The remaining 20 per cent is available to be used at the discretion of the association.

Sales

The Right to Buy scheme under the Housing Act, 1980, as it applies to council tenants, is described in the chapter on council housing. The Government wanted to extend the scheme to housing associations but they objected strongly. They saw no justification for being compelled to sell their stock when their very reason for existence was to own houses which could be let at modest rents. Most associations were registered charities which raised legal and moral problems with sales. The House of Lords agreed with this and the Government gave way. The Right to Buy was confined to tenants of non-charitable associations. In the case of charitable associations, the Government settled for giving them the power to sell if they so chose. Even then, the power would not apply where it was in conflict with the terms of an association's trust. Where associations did sell, the discounts were the same as for council dwellings sold.

Between 1980 and 1984, only 5,309 association houses were sold, about one per cent of the total stock. (In the same period council house sales were 625,775, about ten per cent of the stock). Then the Government tried again. The Housing and Building Control Bill 1984 proposed to extend the sales scheme to all dwellings owned by charitable housing associations. Again, some pressure in the Commons, and very considerable pressure in the Lords, obliged the Government to drop the proposal.

Instead it introduced a scheme for portable discounts called HOTCHA (Home-Ownership for Tenants of Charitable Housing Associations). Tenants whose association refused to agree a voluntary sale at a discount could apply for a grant equivalent to what the discount would have been if the association had been willing to sell. The grant had to be used to assist the purchase of a house on the open market. Only associations nominated by the Housing Corporation could operate the scheme. In its first year only 31 associations (out of more than 2,000) were nominated, and only 159 actual sales were completed.

The Government withdrew the HOTCHA scheme in 1988, and launched a replacement for it in 1990. The Tenants Incentive Scheme (TIS) was similarly aimed at spreading home-ownership and it operated by giving tenants cash grants to enable them to move into the owner-occupier market. The Conservative Government encouraged greater use of TIS and a peak of more than 7,000 grants was reached in 1996/97.

In addition to TIS, the Government re-introduced Do It Yourself Shared Ownership (DIYSO), which was originally launched in 1983. Under DIYSO the tenant continued to rent half their new home and to pay a mortgage on the other half. DIYSO worked on the basis that tenants wishing to move found themselves a suitable house (within specified price limits – which varied from place to place) and their housing association bought the house.

The tenant then paid rent based on half the value and mortgage repayments on the other half. In 1994/95 the DIYSO programme amounted to 4,500 units but declined thereafter. Both TIS and DIYSO were schemes for encouraging housing association tenants to move out and generate vacancies in the rented stock.

In April 1999 the TIS and DIYSO schemes ceased to operate and were replaced by Homebuy. This gives existing RSL tenants an interest free equity loan of 25 per cent of the cost of buying a home (within limits). Homebuy is offered only in areas where there is a shortage of social rented housing to free up an existing dwelling for someone in need. In addition, there is a system of purchase grants available to RSL tenants to assist them to buy their current homes. These grants are significantly less generous than Right to Buy discounts.

The outlook

Until the 1987 White Paper, most people (including the DETR statistics section) saw the housing association movement as part of the public rented sector. Indeed it was more dependent on public funding than council housing. Like council housing, it saw its purpose to provide for people who needed, or preferred, to rent. Its tenants have been as much in need of support from housing benefit as have council tenants.

It was regarded as the voluntary movement at its best: non-profit making; motivated by social considerations; an admirable supplement to council housing; making a particularly valuable contribution to special categories such as the elderly and the single homeless; and widening the choice for would-be tenants. Housing associations have had to come to terms with a very different set of pressures since the 1988 Act. First they had to devise their own rents setting policies after 15 years of not having to worry about rents. At the same time they had to learn about private finance, and to live with the risks involved at a time of rapid expansion in their capital programmes. Later they had to learn to be competitive with each other, in ways that many associations found quite alien to their traditions. More recently they have had to accept severe contraction of their development programmes, closer scrutiny of rents policies and a general tightening of the Housing Corporation's regulatory regime.

It can be argued that housing associations have changed more in the years since the 1988 Act than in any previous period of similar length. The prospects for the foreseeable future are further rapid change, fuelled by the continued formation of new LSVT associations and companies. The impetus behind stock transfer is such that over the next 15 years RSLs might become the second largest tenure category in Britain, behind home-ownership. But if that is to happen it will require huge amounts of money to be raised in private loans. Despite the successes of the last decade, private lenders may not be able to advance the necessary sums at attractive rates. However, if the Treasury were to write off local authority debts, or a proportion of them, stock transfer would continue to attract private finance.

It is already clear that LSVT associations constitute about half of the top 100 associations in Britain by stock size. They will play an important part in the future development of new affordable rented housing whatever the pace of stock transfer over the next few years. The lion's share of new building is carried out by a small group of mostly large associations, a kind of super league accelerating away from most of the smaller associations that have to concentrate on managing their existing stocks. Within the super league there are effectively two distinct groups: the LSVT associations, with housing stocks mainly concentrated within one locality, and whose constitutions attempt to ensure direct accountability to the communities within which they operate, and the large non-LSVT associations. The latter have more dispersed housing stocks, spread over dozens (or even hundreds) of local authority districts. It will be interesting to see whether the distribution of grant aid in future years favours associations in one group or the other.

Another interesting issue will be the fate of the Housing Corporation itself. Hitherto governments have maintained the Corporation as both funder and regulator of associations. There are powerful arguments, however, in favour of funding being devolved to local councils as the strategic housing authorities, or, failing that, to the newly formed Regional Development Agencies in the different parts of England.

Other issues, still to be resolved, concern the ability of RSLs, particularly those with large numbers of old, inner-city rehabilitated properties, to maintain their existing stocks of houses in a decent state of repair. The policies pursued by the Conservatives in the early 1990s made it very difficult for associations to spend the necessary sums on these old houses.

A final point here is about rents and affordability. Governments have been putting pressure on associations to bear down on rents since 1996. It has become increasingly difficult for associations to raise rents to meet necessary expenditure. However, there is an argument for believing that the downward pressure on rents is primarily due to government failure to sort out the housing benefit problem. Once that is resolved the situation might begin to change.

4   The Private Rented Sector

At the outbreak of the First World War, renting was the normal tenure. It accounted for 90 per cent of the housing stock, with only ten per cent owner-occupied, a tiny amount of housing association dwellings, and virtually no council houses. By 1996, following a prolonged decline, private renting in Great Britain had shrunk to 9.8 per cent, as rented dwellings were sold for owner-occupation or became unfit and were demolished. One view of private renting is that it is an essential component of a healthy and responsive housing market. It provides readily available accommodation with none of the complexity faced by house purchasers in terms of the legal costs of property conveyancing, nor the problems and frustration associated with chains of buyers and sellers. Private renting is also there to provide for those households who do not qualify for immediate help by local authorities and housing associations. According to this view it is important to ensure that there is sufficient private renting available. This clearly implies a tax and benefits framework which allows landlords to secure sufficient return on their capital; otherwise they will be likely to move it to where returns are better. At the end of the century there is a certain amount of evidence that more people are expressing a preference for renting privately rather than from a local council or housing association.

Almost 60 per cent of private rented housing was built before the First World War and much of it has suffered from chronic neglect for a very long time. Figures from the latest round of house condition surveys in different parts of Great Britain indicate that by far the worst conditions are found in the private rented sector, where the rates of unfitness are typically three or four times greater than any other sector. This is a shocking state of affairs, and the reasons – largely financial – make a tangled and discreditable story.

In 1915, rents were frozen as a temporary wartime measure and tenants could not be evicted. But tenants were many and they all had votes, and landlords were few. What began as a temporary measure became a permanent feature of housing policy. Other countries had imposed rent control, but none behaved as ineptly as Britain which neither compensated landlords for lost income nor allowed rents to rise as incomes rose. Building for rent was already tailing off before 1914 when other more attractive fields for investment had appeared. Rent control, in the rigid form it took, ensured that investors mostly put their money elsewhere, although nearly a million new privately rented dwellings were added to the stock between the Wars, in the late 1930s. But these were outnumbered by dwellings sold for owner-occupation and demolition. Rent control undoubtedly acted as a severe disincentive to new investment, although there was a certain relaxation of controls and limited rent increases were allowed.

At the start of World War II rent control was re-imposed across the whole of the private sector. It was not until nearly 20 years later that the Conservative Government grasped the nettle of decontrol. The Rent Act, 1957, removed controls on dwellings above certain rateable values and on any property (whatever the rateable value) when a tenant left. This, it was claimed, would halt the decline of the private rented sector by giving landlords a fair return on their investment.

The Government appeared to have completely overlooked that, in conditions of serious scarcity, decontrol would open the door to widespread exploitation. A new word, 'Rachmanism', came into the English language as a result of the activities of one of the more unscrupulous operators in this field. Moreover, instead of stabilising, the sector began to decline faster than ever. As well as giving freedom to increase rents, decontrol ended the tenant's security of tenure, so a landlord could get rid of a tenant and sell with vacant possession. This was a much more attractive proposition than re-letting, even at a high rent. Besides, might not some misguided future government re-impose control?

And this is exactly what happened.

Fair rents

Even before the Conservatives lost the 1964 election, they had become alarmed at the effects of the Rent Act, 1957, and had set up the Milner Holland Committee to examine the Greater London housing problem. They would have had to do something about it if they had been returned to office.

As soon as the new Labour Government took office, it moved swiftly with a temporary holding measure to restore security of tenure and freeze existing rents. When the Milner Holland Committee report appeared in 1965, the Government lost no time. The Minister concerned was Richard Crossman and his problem was that he could not simply return to the old controlled rents which were quite inadequate. Nor could he, in conditions of desperate scarcity, leave rents to market forces. So he devised 'fair rents', a novel and entirely artificial concept designed to allow rents to rise more or less in line with the changing value of money, but under the control of a newly created body of public servants known as rent officers. The Rent Act,

1965 did not define a 'fair' rent, but where landlord and tenant could not agree on the rent level, a rent officer, appointed by the local authority, would decide what a fair rent should be. The Rent Act also provided a return to a greater degree of security for tenants, permitting the creation of regulated tenancies.

In fixing a fair rent the rent officer would ignore the personal circumstances of the tenant but have regard to the age, size, character, locality, and state of repair of the dwelling. The objective was to set a rent which would be fair to both landlord and tenant as if supply and demand roughly balanced – a market rent in the absence of scarcity.

In the early days, most of the applications came from tenants, and the rent officers happily set about reducing large numbers of high rents which had resulted from the 1957 Act. However, dissatisfied landlords or tenants could appeal to Rent Assessment Committees (RACs) appointed by the civil servants. Sir Sydney Littlewood, a well-known valuer, chaired the London Rent Assessment Committee (by far the most important), which set the tone for the other RACs. The London RAC increased many of the rents fixed by rent officers. Thereafter, it was mainly landlords, not tenants who went to the rent officer asking them to set a 'fair' rent for their properties.

Not for the first time, the civil service had defeated the intentions of a minister. Crossman was unhappy but went on claiming that his fair rent idea was basically sound. However, the disquiet was enough for the Labour Government to set up another committee, the Francis Committee, in 1969, to consider how the Rent Act 1965 was working. By the time it reported, two years later, a Conservative Government was in power. The report concluded that although a lot of rent officers found themselves unable to quantify scarcity and therefore made no allowance for it, all was well – though allowing for the effect of scarcity had been the very basis of the Crossman formula. The report was accepted with alacrity.

The Conservative Government went on to pass the Housing Finance Act, 1972. This extended the fair rent concept to council housing and it also made provision for a phased transfer of the remaining old controlled tenancies into the fair rent system called the 'regulated tenancy system'.

This phased transfer was halted temporarily by Labour when it returned to power in 1974, to give itself time to make a full review of the working of the Rent Acts, but it was all change once more, as a Conservative Government took over in 1979.

Effects of the Housing Act, 1980

By 1980, there were 400,000 houses still controlled under the old system. The Conservatives' 1980 Act converted them, at a stroke, to regulated tenancies for which fair rents would be set, whatever the condition of the properties. Landlords would also be allowed to apply for re-registration (for a higher rent) after two years, instead of three. It was the end of the original rent control system which had started in 1915 as a temporary measure.

Two new types of tenancy were also introduced. One was the protected shorthold tenancy, which allowed the landlord to let a vacant property at a fair rent for a fixed term of one to five years and regain possession at the end. It was expected that this would make shortholds an attractive proposition for landlords but it was not particularly successful. They still preferred to sell rather than re-let, since they were not happy with fair rents, even though these were likely to be three times as much as the previous controlled rents. After a couple of years, further legislation provided that, outside London, a landlord need not apply for a fair rent as a condition of letting on shorthold terms.

The other innovation was the assured tenancy. This was a form of tenancy that at first was available only in relation to newly built dwellings provided by landlords approved by the secretary of state. The fair rent system would not apply and rents would be freely negotiated between landlord and tenant. The landlord could let for any period, and at the end of the period the tenant would have a right to a new tenancy on terms to be agreed; or if not agreed, on terms to be settled by the County Court with any rent fixed by the Court at market level. In 1986 the rules were relaxed to allow assured tenancies to be created in existing dwellings if they had been improved or modernised by the landlord, but it was still necessary for landlords to be approved by the secretary of state.

Figure 2

Private renting in Great Britain

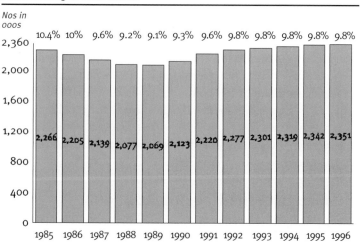

Source:Housing and Construction Statistics

It was claimed that these two new forms of tenancy would at last slow down, and perhaps even reverse, the decline of the private rented sector. But the downward trend continued, as Figure 2 shows.

The Housing Act 1988

In 1987 the Government issued a White Paper setting out its intentions for what was to become the Housing Act, 1988. This was the time when, following their third successive election victory, the Thatcherites appeared to believe that anything was possible, even things that had been unthinkable for decades. Their White Paper covered all tenures, but on the private rented sector the Government proposed to deregulate new lettings while protecting existing tenants. It planned to put new life into what it now calls the 'independent rented sector': housing owned by private landlords and housing associations. Public sector housing would be dispersed to other landlords and the purchase and management of property by the private sector and housing associations would broaden the choice available to tenants.

While protecting the position of existing tenants, the Government proposed to make progress towards market rents by building on the two concepts of assured and shorthold tenancies. The changes made in pursuance of these objectives were set out in the Housing Act 1988, which came into effect on 15 January 1989. For new lettings, the main change was that the regulated tenancy (subject to fair rents) no longer applied. Landlords can choose either:

- *an assured tenancy, with rents freely negotiated but with security of tenure protected – at the end of a tenancy the tenant will be entitled to a further assured tenancy. A spouse will have an automatic right to succeed to the tenancy on the death of the assured tenant. There is no right to a second succession, and other relatives have no right at all to succeed.*

- *an assured shorthold tenancy for which the minimum period for letting has been reduced from one year to six months. There will not be a fair rent, though either party will have the right at any time to get the rent fixed at a 'market level which takes account of the limited security of tenure which the tenant has been offered'. Such a rent will be set by the Rent Assessment Committee.*

Landlords offering assured tenancies no longer have to be approved by the secretary of state, and the basic fitness standard has been abolished. Most of the remaining controls over new lettings by resident landlords (where the landlord lives in part of a dwelling and lets other parts) have been removed.

For tenancies which were in existence before 15 January 1989 the main changes are:

- *the fair rent system still applies, but when a tenancy ends, the landlord can re-let on either an assured or assured shorthold basis.*

- *the spouse continues as the 'protected' tenant, the new description for what was the 'regulated' tenant, when the tenant dies. Other relatives have a right to succeed, but only if they have lived there for the last two years, and only as assured tenants. Second successions are only possible where the person was a member of both the original tenant's family and the first successor's family.*

- *for existing shorthold tenants there is no security of tenure beyond the brief period of the tenancy.*

There are also provisions to protect tenants from harassment by landlords who seek to obtain possession or re-let at higher rents. And landlords are entitled to charge 'key money', for the granting of assured or shorthold tenancies.

Rents and housing benefit for private tenants

Housing benefit is paid by local councils to help private tenants on low incomes with their rents. Council tenants are also entitled to help. This system is described more fully in the next chapter.

Rents rose steeply as 'fair rents' replaced the old controlled rents and did so again after the 1989 deregulation. This was entirely intentional, since the Government's declared aim is to raise rents high enough to reverse the decline of private renting.

Higher rents obviously require higher housing benefit if serious hardship to tenants is to be avoided. The cost to the taxpayer has been substantial. There have been repeated assurances that housing benefit will continue to provide an adequate 'safety net', and the 1987 White Paper (para. 3.18) said that 'the housing benefit system will continue to provide help to those who need it'. But it also said that landlords should not be able to increase the rents of benefit recipients to unreasonable levels at the expense of the taxpayer.

The Housing Act, 1988, requires rent officers to scrutinise the levels of rent which are being supported by housing benefit. When a rent is excessive, the local authority only gets a subsidy on the appropriate market rent. The council, therefore, has to pay benefit based on the rent officer's concept of a market rent, not the landlord's. Not only do the rent officers decide what the market rent should be, they are also required to consider whether the dwelling is too large for the tenant's 'reasonable' needs.

This is a sorry business. For low income tenants, assured rents have come to mean an assurance of more hardship, uncertainty and insecurity. In 1998 it was admitted by the Government that those tenants who were in occupation before January 1989 had been facing excessive rent increases as a result of recent court cases. From February 1999 fair rent increases were linked to the retail price index.

Subsidies for some landlords

In addition to changing the framework for new lettings, the Conservatives also provided a temporary incentive to new investment in private rented housing. This took the form of an extension of the pre-existing business expansion scheme (BES) to cover housing. The scheme had been introduced to encourage the formation of small companies, but in 1988 the then Chancellor of the Exchequer, Nigel Lawson, announced that the rules were to be changed to allow the BES to apply to the provision of rented housing with a ceiling of investment of £5 million instead of the £500,000 which applied to other small businesses. There were limits on the prices of dwellings which could be bought under the scheme – £125,000 in London, £85,000 outside.

Tax relief was given at the marginal rate on investment in any year by an individual of up to £40,000. To increase the incentive in the first few months, the higher marginal rate, 60 per cent, applied if the investment was made by 26 October 1988. Subsequently it was the then marginal rate of 40 per cent.

The practical effect was that with 40 per cent tax relief for example, the investor putting £40,000 into a scheme got a reduction in their tax bill of £16,000; so the investment cost only £24,000. To put it another way, for £24,000 invested there was an added capital subsidy of £16,000. Research carried out by Tony Crook and Peter Kemp (*Housing Studies,* January 1996) showed that more than £3000 million was invested by over 900 BES companies, and that the dwellings provided by entrepreneurial BES companies cost the government £28,000 each in net tax expenditure, equivalent to a subsidy of 48 per cent.

As a further attraction, and to discourage early disinvestment, there was exemption from capital gains tax if the investor left the investment with the BES company for at least five years. The prospect of capital gains was, of course, a very important consideration. Some housing associations and universities set up or linked up with BES companies and agreed to buy the properties or the shares owned by the companies at the end of the five year period. The scheme brought additional private resources into the rented market. It proved to be a good way of generating additional capital and deferring outlay for associations and universities at a time when they were under pressure to expand. It also proved attractive to investors who were certain of recouping their outlay at the end of the period.

The scheme generated 81,000 new dwellings before it was wound up in November 1993. However, housing was explicitly excluded from the Government's replacement initiative. Nevertheless, the scheme did seem to have scored a 'first', breaking new ground by subsidising private landlords who provided rented accommodation for tenants who clearly could afford to be home-owners, but not for tenants who could not.

Other 'perks' for the private landlord

As long ago as 1985, the Greater London Council, just before its demise, did a survey which revealed that the majority of new lets in the London area were evading the Rents Act altogether by devices such as letting on licence, holiday lettings, or simply ignoring the law and operating on a market rent basis. Nothing happened to them, and the 1988 Act gave landlords the green light to raise rents.

A further perk for landlords came with the introduction of the poll tax, in April 1990 (1989 in Scotland). They were mostly charging inclusive rents (ie rent plus rates), and handing over the rates element to the local authority. With the arrival of the poll tax liability fell on each individual and landlords no longer had to hand over part of the inclusive rent. Enterprising landlords simply went on charging as much as before, thus giving themselves a handsome rent increase. The Government's only response to this scandalous business was an expression of pious hope that landlords would behave reasonably.

Can private renting recover?

There is a view that private renting is little more than a relic of the past, which is ill suited to the needs of the present. Regulations that are necessary to protect tenants from arbitrary eviction and from dangerous or poorly maintained accommodation are incompatible with the degree of freedom demanded by landlords. The question that this raises is: do commercial, profit motivated private landlords do anything that not-for-profit registered social landlords could not do better?

The aim of the Conservative Government's policy was to stem, and if possible, reverse the decline in the private rented sector by allowing the charging of market rents for new lettings. Labour in office seems to have adopted a similar line, and the reform of mortgage interest tax relief (see chapter 6) has certainly gone a long way to remove the distortions that previously existed. Decades of policies designed to encourage people into owner-occupation had created a situation in which it was often cheaper to

buy than to rent, and of course there was also the long-term prospect of wealth accumulation through home-ownership. The tax advantages given to mortgaged home-owners helped to inflate property values as a whole, thereby dragging up the rents that landlords needed to obtain, reinforcing the idea that owning was more attractive than renting.

Private renting has been in decline for so long that it is difficult to think of it recovering in the twenty-first century. However, it still accounts for more than two million dwellings, more than twice as many as in the housing association sector. A lot of people are private tenants, and their position needs to be protected. The research by Professors Crook and Kemp led them to conclude in 1996 that despite the Conservative Government's deregulation policies there was still a yield gap, which meant that investors were unlikely to enter the market in significant numbers. However, they noted that reform of tax relief for home-owners would help, and that persistently low interest rates would also contribute. Nevertheless they felt that further assistance to landlords in the form of capital allowances or grants would be necessary. The Conservatives appeared to be moving in that direction in 1995-96. But the Housing Act, 1996, did not in fact make SHG available to profit-seeking organisations, and there seems little prospect of further movement.

5 Housing Benefit

The problem of making an inherently expensive item such as housing affordable can be solved either by lowering the price, by providing a subsidy, or by giving money to consumers so that they can pay the full price. Combining the two approaches is also possible; in housing association schemes, subsidy (SHG) helps to keep rents below the full market level, while most of the tenants claim assistance with their rent through housing benefit (HB). This chapter concentrates on assistance with housing costs, a term which includes both rent and council tax. Council tax is a tax related to the value of the property and levied by the local authority. Together the rent and property tax are the main components of housing costs faced by tenants, and so looking at both is necessary.

HB is a means-tested benefit aimed at tenants with the lowest incomes which is rapidly withdrawn as income rises. HB covers both rent rebates for council tenants and rent allowances for tenants of housing associations and private landlords. Today, most people who rent their homes rely on HB to help them meet their housing costs. The HB system does not apply to home-owners, however low their income might be, although they can claim council tax benefit and some help with mortgage costs through income support or job seekers' allowance. The rules and regulations surrounding the administration of HB are so voluminous and complex that this chapter can aim to give only an outline of the current system. A detailed guide would require far more space than is available here, and in any case there are specialist publications which do the job very well (eg *Guide to Housing Benefit and Council Tax Benefit 1999-2000* by John Zebedee and Martin Ward, Shelter/Chartered Institute of Housing).

Means-tested assistance has only been available to tenants in all tenures since 1972 and HB itself has existed only since 1982. The introduction of HB followed years of debate. In the event, the scheme that was adopted had many shortcomings and was implemented in so short a time-scale that there was considerable administrative confusion. Less than a year after the full scheme started, a review was set up. Important changes were made to HB as part of a wider reform of social security.

The Social Security Act, 1986, led to the introduction of the reformed HB system in April 1988. Further changes took effect from April 1990 (1989 in Scotland), when rate rebates were replaced by community charge benefit. This was not strictly part of housing benefit, since the community charge or poll tax, as it was popularly known, was not a tax on property. With abolition of the poll tax from 1 April 1993, council tax benefit replaced the community charge benefit. The introduction of the council tax meant the restoration of a tax linked to property values after the disastrous excursion into the poll tax, which was levied on all individuals.

The benefits system is subject to almost constant change and review. HB has been changed in some way – excluding annual uprating – on nearly 20 separate occasions since 1994. More fundamental reform is in the offing. In December 1998 the Government issued a consultation paper on proposed changes affecting people in supported housing. This involved the introduction of a transitional housing benefit scheme, pending wider changes in 2003.

Background

The origins of HB lie in debates in the early part of this century about how best to help low income households to afford decent accommodation. The introduction of housing subsidies in 1919 meant that the rents of council houses were generally lower than they would otherwise have been. At first, there was no attempt to ensure that subsidies helped the least well off. Indeed, in the 1920s, the costs of building new houses were so high that even subsidised rents were generally beyond the reach of the poor. Council housing thus began as subsidised housing for the better off skilled workers.

However, in 1930 the Labour Government passed a Housing Act requiring councils to launch slum clearance programmes. Rehousing families from the slums inevitably meant that councils became landlords to growing numbers of poorer people. The Government therefore gave way to demands to provide rent rebates for those who could least afford the rent of a new council house. During the 1930s, both councils and their tenants generally opposed rent rebate schemes and for a while, after the Second World War, interest in providing rebates declined still further. It was in the mid-1950s that a Conservative Government revived debate about the best way to provide help with housing costs. It emphasised the targeting of public resources on those in greatest need. In the mid-50s it urged councils to extend the availability of rent rebate schemes while raising rents generally. There was an important policy shift away from general subsidy and towards means-tested benefits.

However, a very confused and unsatisfactory situation then developed. Local councils continued to have the freedom to choose not to run rebate schemes for their own tenants, and they could design their schemes on any criteria they liked. Meanwhile, the National Assistance Board (replaced by the Supplementary Benefits Commission in 1966) was responsible for providing assistance for people on very low incomes, including council tenants. This led to a long running dispute between the Board and the local authorities, but it also created difficulties for claimants, caught between the two.

The need to resolve this problem intensified after 1972. Local authorities had to provide rent rebates for their own tenants. They had to give rent allowances for private tenants because the abolition of the controlled rents system and the move towards fair rents made the private rented sector less affordable. Before this, there had been no help for private tenants who were working or who, for other reasons, did not qualify for supplementary benefit. Many more tenants now became eligible for benefit.

The parallel existence of the local authority and social security systems also gave rise to what became known as the 'better off' problem. Councils gave rent rebates and rent allowances on a means test which took into account gross income while supplementary benefit operated on a measure of net income. Also, the rebate/allowance scheme was more generous than supplementary benefit to people on higher incomes. This was a recipe for confusion. Although many people qualified for both benefits, they could only receive one. They had to choose whether to claim a rebate/allowance or supplementary benefit but it was often difficult to tell which would make them better off. It was even difficult for skilled housing advisers to decide which benefit people should claim.

The 'better off' problem resulted in hundreds of thousands of people receiving the 'wrong' benefit. This was one of the main reasons for reform which could produce a unified housing benefit. In the late 1970s, the Supplementary Benefits Commission argued for a unified benefit to be administered by the local housing authorities. As well as producing a simpler and fairer system, the SBC wanted it to provide help for low income home-owners who were generally ignored by the existing systems. Home-owners could claim rate rebates, and the few who were entitled to supplementary benefit could be helped with mortgage interest. The system of mortgage interest tax relief was generous to higher earners but treated low income home-owners unfairly.

When the Conservative Government produced its proposals (*Assistance with Housing Costs*, 1981) they largely confined them to administrative reform in all sectors. They spurned the opportunity for fundamental reform of housing finance in favour of a limited reorganisation of responsibilities for the administration of housing benefits plus a certain amount of redistribution towards the poorest at the expense of the slightly better off.

The HB scheme was introduced in two stages, in November 1982 and April 1983, following the Social Security and Housing Benefits Act 1982.

The Times described it as 'the biggest administrative fiasco in the history of the welfare state' (20 January 1984). The complexity of the new system and the speed with which it was introduced, among other things, contributed to this 'fiasco'. Councils were simply not given enough time, nor enough help, to allow them to implement the system successfully. The Government then made a series of cuts in the benefit levels which made it even more difficult for councils and claimants alike.

Initially HB retained the two separate means tests inherited from the old system. After 1982 there were two categories of HB claimants, known as 'standard' and 'certificated' cases. Standard housing benefit was effectively the old rent rebate (or allowance) and rates rebate, while certificated housing benefit was like the housing part of supplementary benefit. People with similar incomes could be treated quite differently depending on whether they were entitled to supplementary benefit or not.

The current housing benefit scheme

A review of the 1982 scheme was completed in 1985 and proposals were incorporated into the Social Security Act, 1986. This Act also reformed other parts of the social security system. Income support replaced supplementary benefit, family credit replaced family income supplement and it introduced the social fund.

The new HB scheme was designed to be simpler to administer and understand: to treat people in similar circumstances in the same way whether or not they were working; to direct help to where it was most needed; to improve accountancy; and to encourage efficient administration.

The new scheme represented an improvement by removing the distinction between standard and certificated cases. All claimants are now assessed on the basis of the income support means test. Although the calculation of benefit entitlement in individual cases is complex, in principle the system is very simple:

- *where a claimant's income is equivalent to, or less than, what is known as the 'applicable amount', then HB provides 100 per cent of eligible housing costs*

- *as income rises above the applicable amount, the level of benefit is reduced. In the jargon of social security, benefit is said to 'taper', and in the case of housing benefit it tapers at a rate of 65p for every £1 of extra income. So, if a person was entitled to HB of £10 per week, they would lose all entitlement when their income reached £16 a week above the applicable amounts after disregards(16 x 0.65 = £10.40).*

For council tax benefit (CTB) the rate of taper is 20 per cent except where a second adult rebate applies, in which case it is 25 per cent. So, a person claiming both HB and CCB would find that their benefit was reduced by 85p for every extra £1 of income. To understand how the scheme works it is useful to look at who can claim HB, how the scheme is administered, how claims are calculated and how benefit is paid. However, some claimants may qualify for second adult rebate instead of main council tax benefit. This is not as common as main council tax benefit and is not covered in this chapter.

The HB scheme applies to both public and private sector tenants. This covers a wide range of landlords, including councils, housing associations, commercial landlords, co-ops and hostels. Home-owners who previously got HB for rates can now only claim the separate council tax benefit but may get help via income support or the job seekers' allowance.

There are two routes to claiming HB and CTB. People claiming income support or job seekers' allowance normally claim HB (and CTB) at the same time from the Benefits Agency or Jobcentre. Anyone claiming income support or job seekers' allowance is given the forms for HB and CTB at the same time. But HB and CTB are administered by the local council so forms have to be passed on to them. The second route to claiming is, therefore, to make a direct approach to the local authority. People not claiming income support usually do this.

Councils must consider several things when assessing a claim. Claimants on income support are easiest to assess because the Benefits Agency will have verified details such as income and capital assets when they assess the income support claim. However, the council still has to investigate the person's rent and council tax, and details of any non-dependent adults living in the same house. People on income support get maximum benefit which covers the eligible housing costs which may not be the full rent due, less any deduction for non-dependants, and 100 per cent of council tax. People not on income support might have to pay significant amounts towards both rent and council tax, depending on their circumstances. However, single people living alone and households with only one adult are entitled to a 25 per cent reduction on their council tax, irrespective of income. To calculate entitlement, the council has to determine:

- *income*

- *capital*

- *the 'applicable amount'*

- *eligible costs*

- *details of any non-dependants.*

Income is calculated on a weekly basis from all sources such as wages, benefits, pensions, and assumed (not actual) interest on savings above £3,000. Some forms of income are disregarded (a small earnings disregard applies where claimants are in employment; the amount depends upon the type of household, and is not proportional to the level of earnings). The term capital applies to savings, property, shares and any lump sum payments from redundancy or retirement. Anyone with more than £16,000 of capital cannot get either HB or CTB but some capital is disregarded, most notably the claimant's home. It is interesting to note that while benefit rates and applicable amounts are regularly uprated, the savings figures have remained unchanged since the third edition of this guide in 1990, despite the effect of inflation.

The 'applicable amount' is the official measure of the amount that people in different circumstances need to meet basic living requirements. The applicable amount for any particular claimant is a combination of the relevant personal allowance plus any relevant premiums. In 1999/2000, the personal allowance for a single person over the age of 25 is £51.40, and for a couple where at least one partner is over 18 and with one child under the age of 11, £114.75. This amount will increase to £119.45 as of October 1999. There are different dependants' allowances for each child in a family. The premiums are extra amounts in recognition of higher costs for certain claimants and households. So, there are premiums for families including lone parents, disabled children, disabled adults, and pensioners.

Eligible costs cover rent and council tax. Different rules, however, apply to different tenures. Since the deregulation of private sector rents in 1989, rent officers have stopped fixing fair rents for new lettings and have started determining market rents for HB purposes (see also chapter four). In cases where the claimant's accommodation is too large, or where the rent is unreasonably high compared with rents for suitable alternative accommodation, the council is not obliged to pay HB on the full rent. The eligible rent then would be set by the rent officer rather than the market. This is an aspect which has been tightened up in recent years.

In January 1996 the Government introduced so-called 'reference rents', to be set by rent officers in relation to the averages prevailing in each area for dwellings of the same size. Where actual rents exceeded the reference rent, the local authority was required to pay benefit on the reference rent plus half the difference. This restriction applied not only to the private sector but also to housing associations. Later in 1996 a further restriction was introduced, namely the 'single room' rent limit for people under 25;

this meant that most single people in this age group were only entitled to HB to cover the cost of a room in a shared house. The Conservatives had planned to extend the single room restriction to cover all single claimants under the age of 60, but the incoming Labour Government scrapped the idea. However, Labour did go ahead with abolition of the 50 per cent top up of benefit in cases where rents exceeded local reference rents.

The final item to be considered is any non-dependants living in the claimant's household. Certain categories of non-dependants are assumed to be making a contribution to the rent and reductions are made in the claimant's HB entitlement, depending on the circumstances of the non-dependant. In 1998 the Labour Government introduced substantial increases in the deductions from HB entitlement for non-dependants.

It is now possible to present an example of a housing benefit calculation, based on a woman (the tenant who is under 60) and her adult son aged 20 living together. Their eligible rent, after deductions, is £50 per week. The mother's take-home pay is £90 and the son's gross pay is £110. They have savings of less than £3,000, and so there is no notional income from interest.

Table 5
Housing benefit calculation

Assessed net income	£ per week	£ per week
£90 less earnings disregard of £5.00)	85.00	
Applicable amount	51.40	
Excess income		
£85.00 less £51.40	33.60	
Housing benefit		
100% of eligible weekly rent		50.00
less non-dependant deduction	16.50	
less 65% of excess income	21.84	38.34
Housing benefit entitlement		11.66

The woman is entitled to £5 earnings disregard as a single claimant, and her applicable amount of £51.40 is the amount for single claimants over 25. Her son is deemed to be contributing £16.50 because he earns between £80 and £117.99 per week.

Turning to a sample council tax benefit calculation, let us consider a family of four people, a couple and their children aged 4 and 20. The mother is not in employment and her only income is £14.40 child benefit.

The father's net pay is £130.00 per week and the eldest child earns £100 gross. The council tax is £650 per annum (see table 6 below)

These are just illustrative, and very straightforward, examples, and different circumstances will give different results. Readers requiring more detailed information should consult the specialist guide mentioned at the beginning of this chapter.

Paying for housing benefit

HB is very expensive in terms of the total cost borne by the Treasury. HB has been increasing as a proportion of the total social security budget ever since the introduction of the revised scheme in 1986. In 1997/98, more than 4.5 million households were claiming benefit, and the cost was £11.5 billion – more than a tenth of the social security spending. In these circumstances it is not surprising that the Treasury is keen to find ways to cap expenditure, and to cream off revenue surpluses generated by local authorities (as discussed in chapter 2). The problem with HB from the Treasury point of view is that total expenditure is demand-led. They must make provision to meet the claims made by all eligible applicants; setting a cash limit on expenditure is not possible. Treasury officials traditionally dislike open-ended expenditure commitments.

The situation is complicated by the fact that, although HB is technically a form of social security, local housing authorities administer it (a few of which contract out the day-to-day running of the service). The cost of rent rebates for council tenants is part of the HRA subsidy. Local authorities receive assistance with the costs of HB in two ways; first, in relation to the cost of benefit paid out, they receive a subsidy equal to 100 per cent for council tenants, and 95 per cent for others. Second, they receive a cash limited grant towards the administrative costs of running the scheme. Councils might not receive full reimbursement for benefits expenditure if they decide to increase their rents by more than the guideline amount set by the DETR. Then they will receive assistance as if they had followed the guideline. If an authority erroneously makes an overpayment of benefit, there is no subsidy payable on the overpayment.

Problems with housing benefit

There are problems with HB at a number of levels. Like any means-tested benefit it is inherently complex and expensive to administer because it requires extensive documentation of entitlement from every claimant. From the claimants' point of view, there are problems about establishing the entitlement to benefit in the first place, and about repeatedly having to renew claims. Complications can arise when people go off benefit for a

Table 6
Council tax benefit calculation

	£ per week	£ per week	£ per week
Assessed net income			
Earnings		130.00	
Child benefit		14.40	
less earnings disregard		10.00	
Total		134.40	
Applicable amount			
couple	80.65		
child under 11	20.20		
family premium	13.90		
Total	114.75		
Excess income £134.40 – 114.75		19.65	
Council tax benefit			
Weekly council tax			12.47
less non-dependant deduction	2.15		
less 20% of excess income	3.93		
	6.08		6.08
Weekly council tax benefit			6.39
Annual council tax benefit			333.10

while and then need to claim again, for example when they are engaged in temporary or seasonal employment. For some people there is the added difficulty of having to try to recover part (or possibly all) of the cost of rent from non-dependants sharing their home. From the point of view of landlords, there are financial and administrative problems, arising from delays in payments coming through from the local authority. The fact that payments are now made monthly in arrears inevitably has an impact on levels of arrears recorded by housing associations concerned about their performance indicators. Housing association tenants can opt to have their HB paid direct to their landlord. This can cause problems if overpayments are subsequently discovered, for the council will seek to recover those overpayments from the association, leaving it to chase the tenant. Overpayments can arise through misunderstanding and mistake but fraud is a possibility. HB fraud is believed to cost the taxpayer hundreds of millions of pounds every year, although no one knows the true figure.

From the Treasury point of view fraud is clearly one of the problems with HB, but there are also structural problems associated with the basic design of the scheme. The British HB system is unusual in that it pays up to 100 per cent of eligible housing costs. Comparable schemes in other countries usually leave tenants with responsibility for a part of their rent.

The drawback of the British system is that, except in cases where the local reference rent is less than the rent being charged, it gives claimants no incentive to bargain with landlords as to the level of rent. Many tenants, therefore, have no incentive to minimise their housing expenditure; since HB is tied to actual rent paid, they cannot increase their non-housing spending power by reducing their rent liability.

Another major criticism of the HB system is that it creates a crippling poverty trap. The very steep rate of withdrawal of benefit and the way that HB interacts with other benefits means that a person moving from benefit into work can lose up to 97 pence of each additional £1 of income. This means that there is very little incentive to take low-paid employment. This in turn is seen as creating distortions in the labour market, not to mention its impact on the cost of welfare. There is no doubt that sorting out the reform of HB is high on the present Government's agenda. Equally, there is no doubt that it is a very hard problem to solve.

The growth of owner-occupation during the twentieth century as a whole, but especially in the last 20 years, has been spectacular. The majority of houses built during the century have been for owner occupation. Transfers from other tenures have also fuelled the growth of the sector – in the past this was mainly from private renting. Since 1980, however, some two million former council houses have become owner-occupied. By 1996 owner-occupation in Great Britain accounted for 16,059 million dwellings, virtually 67 per cent of the housing stock, reflecting its history as the fastest growing and most popular sector. This is not surprising. It is seen to offer the householder more freedom and choice than any other tenure. It has also been regarded as the most profitable investment that ordinary people ever make. In addition, of course, housing policy has been strongly in favour of owner-occupation.

Figure 3

Increase in owner-occupation in Great Britain (000s)

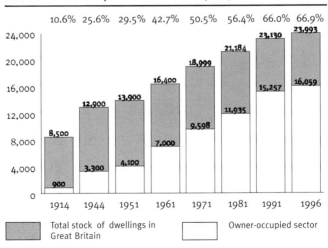

The provision of new housing requires massive amounts of finance. Most purchasers buy their homes with the aid of a mortgage, which is simply a loan secured against the property. However, new construction amounts to only a small proportion of the houses bought and sold in any given year, and most housing market activity involves trade in existing dwellings. The volumes of mortgage finance involved, therefore, are much larger than would be required to fund additions to the stock. Nearly all of this came from building societies until recently. Local authorities, insurance companies and banks made a relatively small contribution. However, enormous changes have taken place since the early 1980s. The high street banks especially have dramatically increased their share of the market. In the mid-1990s there was a major restructuring of the mortgage lending industry. Some of the largest building societies (such as the Halifax, the Woolwich, Northern Rock and Alliance and Leicester) converted themselves into banks. This restructuring has transformed the balance between bank and building society mortgage activity. In 1997 there were only six fewer building societies than in the previous year, but the sector had shrunk by more than half in terms of total assets and numbers of borrowers.

Growth of the building societies

Building societies started in a small way in the late eighteenth century. Small groups of working people joined together, with each member paying a weekly subscription. When there was enough money to buy or build a house, one of the members would take it over, and so on until all had been housed. Each would continue to contribute until all had been dealt with and the group would then disband. These early societies were called 'terminating' societies, and out of their success developed the 'permanent' societies, raising funds by offering a savings bank facility. Building societies developed as mutual societies, borrowing from individual investors and lending to house buyers in what was a closed circuit. They relied to a large extent on small savers, unlike banks, which, as limited companies, issued shares that were tradeable on the stock exchange. Building societies tapped into the growing savings of ordinary people looking for a safe home for their money. After the end of the First World War, the expansion of the building society sector really started. Yet this was as nothing to what followed the Second World War or even the more explosive growth of the last 20 years (see Table 7).

In earlier years there were some colourful characters in the industry and some spectacular episodes involving fraud. But the dramatic success of the last 30 years has been solidly built on a first-rate service to savers and a reputation for reliability. Although mortgage lenders have grown rapidly in terms of the volume of lending for house purchase, there are now many fewer than there were a century ago. In 1900 there were about 2,000 societies but throughout the century the number of societies declined as the size of the industry grew. One factor in this process was mergers as small societies were absorbed into big ones. By the early 1990s, before the conversion of leading societies into banks, there were just 100 societies. Like the housing association sector, a small number of very large societies dominated the business.

Table 7
Building societies' progress

	Advances during year £m	Total assets at year end £m
1900	9	60
1920	25	87
1940	21	756
1960	560	3,166
1980	9,614	53,793
1988	49,376	188,844
1993	31,511	281,152
1997	28,803	137,864

Figures after 1988 exclude Abbey National PLC
Source: Housing Finance, February 1999 (Council of Mortgage Lenders)

The way lenders work

At first sight, the whole basis on which mortgage lenders operate – accepting money which is mostly repayable on demand or at short notice, and lending it for long periods – is the very opposite of what is normally regarded as sound practice. It is borrowing short to lend long. Nevertheless, there is a safeguard which transforms the situation. Each loan is secured by a 'legal charge' on the property: if the borrower fails to comply with the terms of the mortgage, the lender can sell the property and clear the debt from the proceeds of the sale. In this procedure the society is said to foreclose on the loan and to take the house into possession (not repossession).

Traditional building society mortgages contain a 'variable interest clause'. This allows the lenders to make loans for 25 years or even more, although the greatest part of their funds come from investors who are entitled to repayment immediately, or at short notice. When interest rates rise, the lending institution can avoid withdrawals by investors by promptly increasing its own interest rates to investors. It can do this quite safely by giving notice to all its borrowers, under the variable interest clause in their mortgages, that the interest payable will also rise. But in periods of frequent changes in interest rates the societies found that notifying every borrower every time the rate changed was expensive. An increasing proportion of borrowers now find that their repayment changes only once a year, irrespective of movements in interest rates. Building societies take past changes into account when fixing repayments for the coming year.

However, a recent trend has seen the rising popularity of mortgages with interest rates fixed for periods of up to five years. Clearly borrowers are keener to agree fixed interest rates when rates are low, as they have been in recent years. The availability of fixed-rate mortgages has increased because of changes in the way that societies raise their funds. By the end of 1998 half of new loans were at interest rates fixed for more than one year.

In the past building societies raised nearly all their funds from individual investors (often from people saving the deposit to buy their first home). Since the deregulation of financial services in the 1980s things have become much more complicated, and now mortgage lenders raise more of their funds from the money markets.

Deregulation also led to the breakdown of the system of agreed interest rates. The building societies until 1983 published recommended rates of interest to give a measure of stability in a vast financial market which affects millions of people. The members of the Building Societies Association followed the recommendation fairly closely. Since 1983, however, the approach has been different. Each lender fixes its own rates according to market conditions.

Until the early 1980s most borrowers had repayment mortgages, which meant that the loan was paid off gradually over a period. A borrower with a repayment mortgage pays the same amount each month throughout the life of the loan (assuming that interest rates do not change). Each payment consists of two parts: a repayment element and an amount of interest on the loan still outstanding. In the first year payments contain a high level of interest and only a very small amount towards repayment of the principal. But as the years go by, the interest element decreases while the principal element increases and becomes the dominating share of the repayment. The whole calculation ensures that by the end of the period the loan will have been paid off.

Another method, called the low-cost endowment mortgage, became increasingly popular in the 1980s. In this case instead of repaying the principal a little at a time, the borrower takes out a life assurance policy. This provides life cover during the loan period which at the end of the term will yield a sum which will pay off the loan. So the method means paying interest on the whole amount of the loan throughout the loan period, and an annual premium on the assurance policy. It is called low-cost endowment because the borrower reduces the cost of premiums on the life assurance policy by taking out a with profits endowment policy for a sum assured that is less than would be required to repay the loan in full. The profits element (a sort of annual bonus) is expected to more than cover the difference. But there is no guarantee. There have been growing concerns about the capacity of some low-cost endowment schemes to generate enough money to enable borrowers to meet their debts.

By 1981, about a quarter of borrowers were choosing the endowment mortgage; by 1989 it was about 80 per cent but by 1998 the proportion had fallen back to 34 per cent.

One of the largest building societies gives the following examples of the relative costs of repayment mortgages and low-cost endowment mortgages.

Table 8
Typical mortgage costs

	Repayment Mortgage	Low Cost Endowment
Amount of Loan	£60,000	£60,000
Current interest rate (variable)	6.85%	6.85%
Discounted by 2.7%	4.15%	4.15%
Monthly payments		
Net interest	£314.78	–
Net interest	–	£197.13
Life assurance premium	–	£109.94
Optional mortgage protection premium	11.66	–
Total monthly cost	£326.78	£307.07

Figures supplied by the Halifax and based on a £60,000 loan to a couple aged 30.

The figures show monthly repayments net of mortgage interest relief at the rate of ten per cent, on the first £30,000 of the loan. Beyond the £30,000 ceiling no relief is available (this is discussed later in this chapter).

The lending on endowment mortgages is done by the building society, bank or other lender, with the life assurance cover provided by an insurance company. There have been criticisms that the rapid expansion of the method is connected to the fact that lenders, estate agents and solicitors earn a substantial commission from the insurance company on policies sold.

The borrowers

Most would-be home-owners, having found a suitable house, approach a lender for a loan. Lenders used to be prepared to lend 75 per cent, perhaps 80 per cent, of the value of the property. Borrowers would have to find the rest themselves as well as other costs like solicitors' and valuers' fees.

The lender wants to ensure that the borrower will be able to meet the cost of repayments. So for many years a common measure was that a loan could be up to 2.25–2.5 times the borrower's annual income. If there were two incomes involved, usually the second income, or part of it, could be taken into account. Earnings of say £8,000 a year would have been good for a loan of £18,000 to £20,000 if the value of the property justified it.

That was the position until about 1984 but the house price explosion of the late 1980s made for great changes. It led to vastly increased demand for finance from first-time buyers and also from owners who saw an advantage in 'trading up' to larger or better quality dwellings. Incomes were rising too. Building societies and other lenders noted the unprecedented rise in house prices and felt secure in the knowledge that the value of their security (the dwelling) was rising rapidly. They now felt safe in lending three times the annual income. And this was three times a larger income than it would have been two or three years earlier.

Former owner-occupiers re-entering the housing market usually have higher incomes than first-time buyers, and they tend to borrow a lower proportion of the value of their home. In 1998 first-time buyers borrowed, on average, 83 per cent of the purchase price, while former owners borrowed only 64 per cent. When the housing market booms there tends to be an increase in the ratio between average house prices and average wages. This is precisely what happened in the late 1980s when the ratio reached a peak of 4.98, well above the long-term norm of around 3.5. The much more stable housing market of recent years has seen the ratio fall back to more manageable levels. Falling interest rates in the late 1990s have also made access to home-ownership more affordable than it was ten years ago. The changing mortgage market has also allowed borrowers to shop around for the best buys. By the end of 1998, more than a third of the new loans were the result of people remortgaging their existing homes to secure a better deal.

Subsidies for owner-occupiers

In the past there was a running debate about which tenure was the most heavily subsidised. The subsidies to council housing were transparent and easily measured. However, in the case of owner-occupation, some people argued that there was no subsidy at all, while others pointed to the value of tax relief on mortgage interest. Alongside this there was an obscure academic debate about what was the proper way to define and measure the subsidy to owner-occupation. Public attention, however, focused on the rising cost of tax relief and its very inequitable distribution, with the greatest help going to those on highest earnings. During the 1980s Mrs Thatcher virtually single-handedly resisted growing demands from housing analysts and the Treasury for reform of mortgage interest relief. As recently as the 1992 general election the Conservative manifesto pledged the Party to a continuing commitment to mortgage interest relief. The political importance of the votes of home-owners made it difficult for any party to campaign for the reform of the mortgage interest relief system.

Schedule A tax

The ownership of property always used to be taxed on its rental value. The tax was called Schedule A tax, as distinct from Schedule D which is levied on profits, or Schedule E on earnings.

Owner-occupiers do not pay rent. Of two people in identical houses, worth a rent of say £2,000 a year, one owning and one renting, the owner will have £2,000 a year more to spend than the one who is a tenant. It has been argued that the owner has sacrificed income by putting money into buying a house instead of investing it in some other way. That is perfectly true. But if the money had been invested so that it produced £2,000 annual income there would have been tax to pay on that income; whereas no tax is payable on the increase in disposable income which results from owning instead of renting.

In 1955, a Royal Commission on the Taxation of Profits and Income recommended that taxation of the benefit of ownership (on what it called the 'imputed rental') was right, and should continue as an essential element of a fair taxation system.

Nevertheless, in 1962, the Chancellor announced the abolition of Schedule A income tax on owner-occupied houses. Since then, owners have enjoyed tax-free increases in net disposable income as compared with what happens to tenants. They are being given favourable treatment by being

Table 9
Loan advances for house purchase

	No. of advances	Average income of buyer	Average dwelling price	Average advance	Advance as % of dwelling	Advance times income
	000's	£	£	£	%	
First time buyers						
1987	355	4,800	10,857	8,515	78.4	1.8
1988	580	13,990	35,807	30,374	84.8	2.2
1993	305	17,981	47,597	38,801	81.5	2.16
1998	527	22,713	61,344	50,921	83.0	2.24
Former owner-occupiers						
1987	382	5,558	16,246	9,101	46.0	1.6
1988	650	17,108	61,540	36,013	58.5	2.1
1993	259	24,492	77,284	50,124	64.9	2.05
1998	565	31,693	101,250	64,918	64.0	2.05

Source: Housing Finance (CML) No42 May 1999

relieved of tax which should be paid if there is to be tax neutrality between one taxpayer and another. It is important to remember here that tax breaks given to particular groups mean that taxpayers generally have to pay more to make good what is lost.

Tax privileges for owner-occupiers

A householder, while the legal owner, might not own outright, if the property is still on a mortgage – nearly half of all home-owners are still paying off their mortgages. There is ownership in a legal sense but, in practical terms, the householder is only in the process of becoming the owner, not yet enjoying the full benefits of ownership. It would clearly not be equitable to tax mortgagors as if they did own outright. They are saving themselves a rent but they have to meet repayments on a mortgage.

Before the abolition of Schedule A tax, tax relief on mortgage interest was not a problem. In accordance with normal taxation practice, mortgagors were entitled to set off the expense incurred in acquiring an asset against any tax levied on income arising from ownership of that asset. So when Parliament abolished Schedule A tax, there remained no logical reason for giving tax relief on mortgage interest, except as an inducement to people to buy houses on a mortgage.

There is nothing wrong in principle with assisting home-ownership. What had been wrong, and dishonest, was the constant stressing of the heavy cost of subsidies to council tenants as if these increased the burden on the taxpayer whilst tax concessions to owner-occupiers did not. The situation became worse year after year. Housing subsidies for rented houses were reduced while the cost of tax relief for house purchase increased at an alarming rate. The cost, as reported by ministers, was the gigantic sum of £7,700 million in 1990/91 for relief on mortgage interest alone. The cost of relief fell to £1,900 million in 1998/99, reflecting lower mortgage interest rates and progressive reductions in the level of assistance available. Until 1991 higher rate tax payers had been entitled to mortgage interest relief at the higher rate, although people who earn enough to be higher rate tax payers are more able to meet their housing costs without subsidy. The cost of relief was further reduced from April 1994 by the decision to cut the rate at which relief is given to 20 per cent; further cuts brought the level of help down to ten per cent by 1998, by which time the average borrower was receiving just £180 per year. In the budget of March 1999 the Chancellor made the historic announcement that tax relief would disappear altogether in April 2000.

The huge overall cost of interest relief in the early 1990s was due to the rapid increase in the number of mortgaged home-owners in the late 1980s, the very high interest rates in 1990/91 and the prevalence of endowment

89

WHY? BECAUSE I'M WORTH IT..
YOUR TAX PRIVILEGES, SIR
TAX MAN
TRADESMANS' ENTRANCE

mortgages (which maximise entitlement to assistance). For individual home-owners, however, a number of factors diminished the value of relief. First, relief is only available on the first £30,000 of any mortgage, and this ceiling has not been increased since 1983. At that time the average new mortgage was £18,350, and by 1994 the average was £48,600. Second, falling income tax rates meant that tax relief also fell – in 1979 the basic rate of tax was 33 per cent compared with 25 per cent in the mid-1990s; for the rich the top rate of tax has been cut from 83 per cent in 1979 to 40 per cent now.

Before 1983, mortgagors got tax relief on mortgage interest by a reduction in their tax bill up to a permitted maximum. Someone liable only for tax at the standard rate got relief at the standard rate. Someone who paid tax at a higher rate got relief at the top rate.

In April 1983 the system was changed by the introduction of MIRAS (Mortgage interest relief at source). Mortgagors paid interest reduced by tax at the standard rate, and the Exchequer reimbursed the building societies for lost income. This finally nailed the argument that tax relief was not a subsidy.

The sale of any asset normally results in liability to capital gains tax on any profits from the sale. Home-ownership, where the home is the principal dwelling of the seller, is exempt. The Inland Revenue estimated the cost of this exemption to be worth £1,350 million in 1998-99.

Ownership has, therefore, been seen as a very good hedge against inflation. The house buyer's costs are mainly mortgage repayments and these are fixed, not on the current value of the dwelling, but on the amount borrowed when the house was bought. It is this characteristic of home-ownership – annual costs based on the historic cost – that is its most important and valuable feature, but only when prices are rising.

No wonder home-ownership has been highly regarded, and continues to be, despite the ravages of the slump in house prices in the early 1990s.

Other considerations

Since the bursting of the house price bubble in 1988 we have seen another side to home-ownership. People have learnt through bitter personal experience that home-ownership is not a guaranteed route to wealth accumulation. A new term – negative equity – entered the language. People who had bought houses with high percentage mortgages, when prices were high, found that falling prices left them with debts which exceeded the value of their homes. The Bank of England estimated that negative equity affected one million home-owners in 1992, although others have put the figure at nearer 1.5 million.

Negative equity becomes a problem for borrowers when they want to sell their houses. The recession of the early 1990s threw large numbers of people out of work. Increasing numbers of borrowers found that they could neither afford to meet their mortgage repayments nor sell at a price that would cover the outstanding debt. The dream of home-ownership had turned into a nightmare for people who were simultaneously victims of both housing policy and economic recession.

Mortgage arrears of more than six months rose during the 1980s, but really accelerated in the early 1990s. By 1992 more than 350,000 borrowers were more than six months behind with their mortgage payments. Not surprisingly the lenders, which are, after all, commercial financial institutions, began to increase the rate at which they took houses into possession. In 1989 15,810 houses were taken into possession. In the following year the figure jumped to 45,890 and rose to an all time record of 75,540 in 1991. Since then things have improved somewhat and the levels of mortgage arrears have come down. However, the severity of the housing market slump following the absurdities of the boom must surely have dented people's faith in home-ownership. This may be a good thing if it helps to lower expectations and prevent the sort of speculative activity that led to the problems. The apparent trend towards low inflation and low interest rates can also be expected to change attitudes to debt.

In inflationary times, there are advantages in being a borrower. Debts are repaid with devalued pounds and, as inflation pushes up incomes, so the burden of debt repayments quite rapidly diminishes. This was one of the factors that helped to make owner-occupation so attractive for so long. However, if inflation remains at very low levels then taking on a large mortgage will imply permanently heavy debt repayment burdens. Both borrowers and lenders can be expected to adjust their behaviour accordingly.

7 Reform

Previous chapters have revealed something of the complexity and inconsistency of British housing finance arrangements. This chapter looks at the case for reform and assesses its impact on government policy up to the change of government in 1997. The next chapter concentrates on the present period and the prospects for change and/or reform under Labour.

Over the years there have been numerous calls for reform, and governments have repeatedly changed policies on pricing, subsidy and taxation but not necessarily in line with the demands of reformers. Some people have argued for coherent, across the board reform because existing arrangements are inequitable, while others have given priority to the removal of distortions in the housing market. Governments have been more interested in using housing finance for restructuring the pattern of tenure – specifically to increase demand for home-ownership, and to attack council housing. The politics of housing and wider economic considerations have also constrained progress on reform. It was widely believed that it was politically impossible to reform mortgage interest tax relief, even though it was expensive and inequitable, because too many voters were benefiting from it.

The idea that housing finance arrangements in Britain were in need of fundamental reform came to prominence in the early 1970s. The first signs of the instability that became such a feature of the housing market over the next 20 years emerged at that time. Massive increases in house prices focussed attention on the cost of mortgage interest tax relief, and established that tax relief was really a form of subsidy to house buyers. The Conservative Government of the day launched what it referred to as a fundamental reform of housing finance. They introduced via the Housing Finance Act, 1972, a set of changes in the rental sectors which mainly involved controversial rent increases for council tenants. The glaring inequity in the distribution of assistance to home-owners remained untouched.

The Labour Government was elected to power in 1974. It repealed the most contentious parts of the 1972 Act, and set up a Housing Finance Review. They initially billed this as an attempt to tackle the 'dog's breakfast' that was British housing finance. The review led to very little, apart from the outline of a new subsidy system for council housing. There was also a positive rejection of the need for reform in the owner-occupier sector, and an endorsement of the existing arrangements, including tax relief.

The election of a Conservative Government in May 1979 ushered in what was to become 18 years of Tory rule, giving the party time to stamp its distinctive mark on housing finance. It is instructive, therefore, to look at how the reform lobby (or lobbies) fared under Thatcherism and post-Thatcherism, and at what the Tories did in practice to change the system.

The case for reform

The case for reform has been that housing finance in Britain has developed over a long time without any clear or coherent set of principles holding it together. Short termism and political expediency led to arrangements that were inconsistent, inequitable, inefficient, ineffective and needlessly complicated. Different tenures have different tax and subsidy regimes, so that there is inequity among households according to the type of tenure that they choose. There is also inequity among households within tenures. Pricing and subsidy systems have been accused of distorting the pattern of demand.

Housing finance systems should be designed to meet a number of basic objectives, against which they can be evaluated. The conventional objectives of housing policy, covering quantity, quality and price suggest that sufficient investment should be made to ensure an adequate supply of housing, at prices (whether to rent or buy) that enable everyone to have access to a socially acceptable standard of accommodation (ie, no one should have to live in accommodation that is overcrowded, in serious disrepair or lacking in basic modern amenities). In addition, it is important that subsidies are equitably distributed, targeting help on those in need. There is also a strong case for saying that the financial framework should not lead people to choose one tenure rather than another.

In Britain at the present time there is inadequate investment in both new building and in the maintenance of the existing stock. Most independent estimates suggest that there is a need for around 100,000 new rental dwellings each year. However, output by local authorities has been cut back to nothing, and cuts in the Housing Corporation budget mean that housing association production falls far short of the required total. In the private rented sector there have been claims of a revival of investment in new supply, but no one seriously expects this to amount to very much overall.

Turning to the quality of the stock, it has been estimated that one dwelling in thirteen is unfit for human habitation. *'For owner occupied, privately rented and housing association homes the outstanding costs of meeting the comprehensive repair standard expected by building societies for mortgage purposes is at least £46 billion*' (P Leather, S Mackintosh & S Rolfe, *Papering Over the Cracks*, 1994).

Affordability has been much debated in recent times, although governments have steadfastly refused to say clearly what is an affordable level of household expenditure on housing. The evidence shows that rents in all sectors rose much faster than inflation in the first half of the 1990s. Government policy has since swung round to an emphasis on low rent increases.

Targeting of subsidy has improved in recent years as income related assistance has come to replace general (bricks and mortar) subsidy. However, serious problems are now arising from the deep poverty trap generated by the way that benefit is withdrawn as income rises. Higher rent levels mean that people living on benefits suffer from powerful disincentives to find work.

There are three basic questions to be considered in the construction of a coherent housing finance system:

- *What should people pay for their housing?*

- *How can they be helped to afford suitable housing?*

- *How should the financial benefits of house ownership be taxed?*

In practice the pricing question comes down to debate about the principles for rent setting (given that no one seriously proposes to interfere with market pricing in owner-occupation): should there be one pricing policy for all rented housing, and if so what should it be based on? Should the market set rents for all, including local authority and housing association tenants?

The question of subsidy arises because of the inherently high cost of housing and the undesirable social and economic consequences of a section of the population living in unhealthy housing. But should subsidies be applied to the prices (rents) or to the incomes of individual occupiers? Price subsidies are open to the criticism that they are indiscriminate and wasteful, often benefiting people who could afford to pay the full price. Income subsidies are better targeted and likely to produce less distortion of overall demand. Income related, means-tested benefits, however, have their own drawbacks. They are complex and expensive to administer, open to abuse and can lead to labour market distortions if people find little improvement in moving from benefit into employment. The debate about a general subsidy or targeted housing benefit type subsidy has been going on for many years. Following a strong tide in favour of targeting, there has been a return to government support for general subsidy since 1995 .

The issue of taxation is complicated by the question of whether housing should be treated as an investment, and therefore taxed in the same way as other investment goods. Most economists believe that it should be regarded and taxed in this way. This then leads to the argument that home-owners earn two sorts of benefit from their investment, both of which should be taxed, as are gains from other sorts of investment. First, home-owners are deemed to have received what is called imputed rental income (as mentioned in chapter 6). This is easiest to understand by thinking about a different situation in which a person owning a house lets it to tenants. In this case they would be liable for tax on the rental income. The argument for taxing the imputed rental income of owner-occupiers is that as investors they are renting their house to themselves as consumers. The fact that no money changes hands does not mean that it cannot be taxed. Second, home-owners generally expect to accumulate wealth through the increase in the value of their property over time. Capital gains arising from the ownership of other sorts of durable assets are liable for tax, and gains from investing in housing could also be taxed.

The case for seeking some common, across the board, approach to rent setting, and for taxing home-ownership, is that of tax and tenure neutrality. The principle of neutrality is that fiscal considerations should not influence decisions about type of tenure, or about whether to invest in housing or shares. In practice people have been encouraged to invest in owner-occupation because of its privileged tax position. There is no taxation on both imputed rental income and capital gains, and there has been tax relief on income used to pay mortgage interest. In rented housing, subsidies to councils and housing associations but not to private landlords (apart from the temporary BES episode) distort demand as tenants respond to rents at sub-market levels in the social rented sector. This implies that the market should set the baseline for rent setting, or something close to the market. If the result is rents that are beyond the reach of low income households then that can be dealt with by some sort of income related housing allowance.

Moving from these kinds of considerations to actual reform proposals is not straightforward. It would be politically very difficult to introduce a tax on imputed rental income. In practice most reform proposals have concentrated on the removal of mortgage interest tax relief instead. Many people have put forward blueprints for the reform of housing finance in Britain – as long ago as 1991 John Hills identified 19 sets of proposals between 1978 and 1989. It is not appropriate to try to look at these here, but it is instructive to look at the package with the highest profile, to understand the kinds of suggestions that were on the table, and to look at how the government responded.

The Duke of Edinburgh's Report

In July 1985 there was a major contribution to the debate from a committee set up by the National Housing Federation and chaired by the Duke of Edinburgh. The *Inquiry into British Housing* attracted wide attention, much of it directed to one recommendation, that mortgage interest relief was not justified and should be phased out. This was a pity, for it was only one of several equally important proposals. The value of the report was in its comprehensive survey of the situation, the arrangements which had produced it and the challenging solutions that were proposed. It recommended a tenure neutral housing finance system based on the phasing out of mortgage interest tax relief and the introduction of a needs related housing allowance and capital value rents in all rented sectors.

The needs related allowance was intended to replace the tangle of subsidies, housing benefit and mortgage interest tax relief. It was designed to extend to low income owner-occupiers, who are not eligible for housing benefit.

The Inquiry recommended that tenants in all sectors should pay rents based on four per cent of the current capital value of their home (assuming vacant possession) plus an allowance for management and maintenance. This would give comparability across all rented dwellings, and while rents would be set to give a reasonable return they would not be as high as in an unregulated market. It was claimed that rents set on this basis would be sufficient to attract new capital investment into private renting.

Capital value rents would result in big increases for many tenants and it was accepted that the introduction of the needs related allowance was a necessary precondition of the new approach. Indeed the recommendations of the Inquiry team were clearly set out as a package:

'Our central recommendations hang together as a unity: they are not a checklist from which some parts, but not others, can be extracted.' (page vii)

The Report criticised successive governments for making piecemeal decisions and failing to face the challenge of coherent, across the board reform. The insistence of the Inquiry team that their proposals were to be taken as a package contributed to the Government's decision instantly to reject them. The Government of the day (and probably most governments most of the time) preferred to pursue its radical objectives by revealing only one step at a time. Committing itself to a complex package of fundamental reforms was too risky. The other main reason was the inclusion within the package of the phasing out of mortgage interest tax relief. This was then politically unacceptable to the Prime Minister, Margaret Thatcher, who remained personally committed to its retention right up to her departure from office in 1990.

The Duke's Second Report

In 1990 the Inquiry team reconvened and after further deliberation published a second report in June 1991. The second report essentially relaunched the package of proposals contained in the 1985 report. It also went on to argue for a series of further measures designed to reverse the continuing decline in the overall availability of rented housing. In the local authority sector the Report called for recognition that the ring-fencing of the housing revenue account had changed the relationship between housing and other local services. The logic of treating the landlord function as separate from other local authority accounts dictated that the government should go further and treat local authority landlords in a similar way to independent housing associations. This would give local housing authorities freedom to raise private finance, secured against the value of the stock.

However, the Report recognised the difficulties of challenging the rigid Treasury conventions on public expenditure. It went on to suggest that it might be necessary to introduce 'transfers of engagements' to get round the restrictions. This would mean transferring the ownership of all the assets and liabilities of the housing stock to financially independent bodies. The idea of 'local housing companies' was followed up in a report commissioned by the Joseph Rowntree Foundation.

The Duke's Second Report also suggested an end to the system, introduced in the Local Government and Housing Act, 1989, by which housing benefit payments made to local authorities for their tenants are reduced by notional HRA surpluses. This was a welcome recognition of the fact that housing benefit is a social security payment, not a housing subsidy. Private landlords and housing associations receive rental income based on full payment of housing benefit, and only local authorities are penalised in this way.

Taken together the two reports of the Inquiry into British Housing represent a major contribution to the debate about the reform of housing finance. However, their impact on government policy was negligible – proof that to bring about change in policy it is necessary to have more than a convincing set of arguments. Even proposals emerging from a panel of highly respected, independent and well-connected experts failed to make any headway with a government that was intent on following its own course.

Housing and the Economy

It is important to recognise that governments have to take into account factors that can be set aside by single issue pressure groups. Most obviously governments cannot ignore the impact on voters of unpopular reforms. But they also have other concerns, such as the control of public expenditure and the overall management of the economy. This includes taking into account the knock-on effects from reform on, for example, expenditure incurred by other government departments, and activity in the labour market. In addition, governments find it convenient to use financial mechanisms to control or at least steer the decisions of local authorities.

One of the most important developments in the debate about housing and the reform of housing finance in Britain during the Conservative years was growing recognition of the significant links between housing and the wider economy. This was an area where Shelter played an influential part in taking the analysis of academic economists to a wider audience. The wild fluctuations in the economy, and even more marked ups and downs in the housing market in the 1980s undoubtedly stimulated much of this work. After 1979 the Government stoked up demand for home-ownership, so that by the end of the 1980s two-thirds of the population were in this tenure. At the same time the Government set about deregulating financial services, making it much easier to obtain credit. The deregulation of banking in the early 80s led to the ending of the building societies' interest rate cartel, ending mortgage queues, and leading to the Building Societies Act, 1986. With real incomes rising as the economy recovered from the recession of 1981 there was strong upward pressure on house prices. As people saw the value of their assets increase so they were encouraged to turn their wealth into increased demand for consumer goods.

The combination of larger numbers of home-owners and much increased house values created a vast amount of unused equity. It dramatically increased the importance of the housing market in the economy as a whole. Economists such as John Muellbauer provided powerful explanations of what was happening. Muellbauer argued that by letting house prices rise so fast in 1986-88 the Government committed one of the biggest blunders of economic management in the whole of the postwar period – which is saying something!

Muellbauer added his voice to those calling for the reform of mortgage tax relief, suggesting what he called a self-financing system. Entitlement to relief would be limited to the first eight to ten years of a loan. The cost of this would be covered by a tax levied on home-owners with more mature loans. He also suggested that lenders should provide lower proportions of purchase prices and that home loans should be given a higher risk rating. Subsequent experience has shown this to be entirely justified. This would require purchasers to save bigger deposits and help to prevent the kind of mad rush to borrow that occurs when housing markets are booming.

The importance of the work by Muellbauer and others is that it draws attention to the need for policy makers to recognise that the housing market has great influence on the economy, and vice versa. This did a lot to raise the prominence of housing in public debate.

Much change, little reform

The Conservative Government did not embrace the idea of reform in housing finance as it was understood by academics and lobbyists, and was openly scornful of some of the proposals put forward. But that does not mean it neglected the issue; on the contrary, successive Conservative governments were actively involved in legislating on many aspects of housing finance. There were:

- *two new subsidy systems for council housing*

- *two attempts to recast the rent rebate (housing benefit) system*

- *new controls on local authority capital expenditure*

- *a new financial regime for housing associations*

- *deregulation of private renting*

- *an experiment with tax breaks for investors in private renting*

- *major changes to the financial environment within which building societies operate and, at last,*

- *a real breakthrough on the issue of mortgage interest relief.*

What needs to be appreciated here is that all these changes did not add up to a coherent reform of housing finance based on a commitment to greater equity and efficiency. But neither were they completely incoherent – Tory governments did know what they were doing. Three main factors drove their housing finance policies. First, they were deeply committed to the rapid growth of home-ownership, partly because they believed in the virtues of private market solutions to all problems, and partly because of a crude party political calculation that more home-owners meant more Tory voters. As a result of this commitment the reform of housing finance was anti-council housing. It was tilted in favour of reinforcing demand for home-ownership rather than constructing a system that was equitable, economically efficient and tenure neutral. This is why the reform of tax relief was so staunchly resisted by Margaret Thatcher for so long.

Second, there was a consistent preference for personal, income related subsidies over bricks and mortar subsidies, in both the council and housing association sectors. This was itself related to the wish to move rents in all sectors towards market levels, to help revive private renting.

Third, housing policies were heavily influenced by the Treasury and its attempts to control or reduce public expenditure for many years. The importance of the Treasury cannot be overstated in this context, and housing policy, like other programme areas, was heavily Treasury driven in the main. When the Government at last moved to reduce tax relief in the early 1990s, their intention was to reduce the overall budget deficit, and not to redistribute resources into a fairer mortgage benefit system.

8 | What next?

Labour's inheritance

Eighteen years of Tory rule produced considerable change in housing finance, creating at least as many problems as it has solved. In many ways the housing situation is worse now than it was in the late 1970s. The sale of council houses and the forced ending of new building by local authorities have led to a huge reduction in the supply of rented accommodation. Constraints on repairs expenditure have added to the huge backlog of work, and helped to intensify the difficulties associated with parts of the council sector.

Policies designed to shift the subsidy burden from bricks and mortar to personal assistance have created savage poverty trap problems for millions of low income households. A government which reduced the top level of tax for the rich to 40 per cent had raised the 'tax' rate applied to some people moving from benefit into work to 97 per cent. The Party of incentives and individual responsibility eliminated all work incentives for the poorest and reinforced the very dependency that it sought to remove.

Pushing the housing associations into the grip of private financial institutions forced rents to rise and threatened the long-term viability of associations as effective developers of new affordable rented housing. Despite all the efforts of the Government to revive private renting, it was the collapse of the owner-occupier market after 1988 that eventually led to a measurable increase in supply in this sector.

Housing policy under the Conservatives was undermined by the obsession with home-ownership as the solution to most problems, blind faith in the power of market forces and the belief that private enterprise is always superior to public services. The unending and unjustified assault on local government and the retention of irrational public spending conventions only made matters worse.

Labour in office

At numerous points in this book we have been severely critical of the Tory record in government. But what of the Labour Government? The size of its majority suggests that it is unlikely to be defeated at the next election. There is time to think through, and implement the thoroughgoing reform that has been needed for so long. However, there is no sign that Labour is any more interested in comprehensive packages of tenure neutral housing finance reform than were the Conservatives. And for much the same reasons, Labour too would rather proceed one step at a time, despite repeated references to joined up thinking. It is more concerned with managing the economy and regenerating rundown neighbourhoods than with the design of elegant housing finance systems.

In the run-up to the general election, the Party's strategy was to make as few promises as possible. However, Nick Raynsford, the Shadow Housing Minister made several explicit pledges. An end to compulsory competitive tendering for council housing management, the release of local authorities' accumulated capital receipts and a return to the rights enjoyed by homeless people before the Housing Act, 1996, were all clear commitments. In practice, of course, Hilary Armstrong, not Raynsford, became the first Labour Housing Minister for nearly 20 years. In the short term, Labour's election strategy of committing themselves to staying within the Conservatives' spending plans for the first two years left little room for dramatic gestures. During 1997-98, however, Labour allowed a small increase in the amount of capital spending by local authorities, thus beginning to fulfill the promise to release capital receipts.

As a substitute for immediate action the Government launched a series of comprehensive spending reviews (CSR), covering all the main programme areas. The results of the CSR were announced in July 1998. Although the headlines were grabbed by education and health, housing spending by local authorities was increased by £3.6 billion over three years. This, in effect, completed the release of capital receipts. Housing associations saw their planned expenditure held more or less constant. However, it is important to remember that even after this injection of money, councils will be spending less than they were in the early 1990s. Labour has a long way to go to restore expenditure on council housing to a satisfactory level.

From subsidy to taxation

Throughout this book we have discussed the various ways in which housing has been, and is, subsidised. For much of the twentieth century debates about subsidy – how much, to whom and on what basis – have been central to the politics of housing. But at the very end of the century a new and very different situation is emerging. The national housing revenue account for council housing has been in surplus for several years, leading to controversy about the ownership and control of cash surpluses at local level. With the abolition of mortgage interest tax relief in April 2000, and the simultaneous increase in stamp duty on transactions at the top end of the housing market, owner-occupiers will be taxed rather than subsidised for the first time in years. If the current low rates of mortgage interest turn out to be the norm in the future then there is arguably less need for subsidy. The Government may also have to find some alternative to interest rates to regulate the market if prices start to rise too steeply.

Economic management that avoids the disastrous cycle of boom and slump which caused so much damage to the housing market in the past would represent major progress. Economic stability could lead to greater stability in house prices. This might encourage people to think of their houses more as homes for living in and less as wealth generating investments. Exactly what is going to happen in the British housing market is very difficult to predict, largely because of the uncertainty about whether and when Britain joins the Euro, and about what the impact of joining would be. However, it is worth noting that European countries tend to have lower mortgage interest rates than in Britain, but they pay more in property taxes.

Rents

Policy on rents has been subject to sharp changes of emphasis over recent years. There is still a need for an agreed long-term approach that allows landlords to invest without rents becoming unaffordable for tenants. In the housing association sector the deregulation of rents in 1989 was understood to be a necessary condition for private finance to work. However, more recently, governments have tightened their control over rent increases without loud complaints by the lenders. If associations are to meet their investment obligations (especially in relation to stock re-generation) and achieve high standards then it will be very difficult for them to keep rent increases below inflation.

As to the ambition to standardise rent levels and rent setting procedures across housing association and council sectors there is no real evidence that this laudable objective is any nearer achievement. The Government is much more likely to give priority to resolving the problems in housing benefit.

Housing benefit

The reform of housing benefit has been urgently required for more than a decade, but it is fiendishly difficult to sort out. The Labour Government has already lost two ministers involved with social security reform. Housing benefit reform is the really big issue to be tackled over the next few years. At the time of writing, the Government has revealed that it intends to publish a Green Paper on housing and housing benefit, but none of the

details are yet available. As so often, it is easier to describe the problem than to predict the particular solution that the civil service will come up with.

Stock transfers

The return of a Labour Government means that local authorities are working in a less hostile environment, but Labour's modernisation agenda means that there can be no return to the ways of the past. In particular, the increased funds available to councils are directed towards refurbishment of existing houses rather than the construction of new ones. Labour has refused to listen to the demands for reform of the Treasury's public expenditure conventions that prevent local authorities from borrowing against the value of their housing stock. One factor in this may be that the Government wants councils to press ahead with transferring their housing to other landlords. The increased stock transfer programme for 1999/2000 suggests that there will be no let-up in the remortgaging of council housing via transfer to new ownership.

And finally

The Labour Government under Tony Blair's leadership has already shown that it is a reforming government willing to contemplate measures of far-reaching significance. The announcement of the introduction of resource accounting is just one example. We can expect further rapid change over the next few years, partly arising from internal developments such as the devolution of housing to the parliament in Edinburgh and the assembly in Cardiff, and partly from external sources in the EU.

Index

How many homes will we need?
The need for affordable homes in England.

Specially recommended to academics, policy makers and housing planners.

With the rapid approach of the year 2000, Shelter has commissioned a long-term research project with a view to achieving a decent home for every household at an affordable price. The findings will be published in four separate reports.

How many homes will we need?:

- provides a comprehensive assessment of housing need at the national level

- illustrates how the national figures translate into regional and local pressures

- analyses how the cost of adequate housing varies between tenures and regions

- sets out the implications of current conditions for access and affordability

Please send me _____ copies of *How many homes will we need?* at £12.50 plus 75p postage & packaging

☐ I enclose a cheque/postal order (payable to 'Shelter') for £_____

☐ Please debit my Credit/Delta/Switch card

Card No: ☐☐☐☐ ☐☐☐☐ ☐☐☐☐ ☐☐☐☐

Expiry date: ☐☐☐☐ Start date: ☐☐☐☐ Issue No: ☐☐
(Switch/Delta)   (Switch/Delta)

Name: _____

Address:_____

_____

Postcode: _____ Tel: _____

Please photocopy this form and return it to:

Shelter Publications
88 Old Street
London EC1V 9HU
Or fax: 020 7505 2030
Visit Shelter's website at http://www.shelter.org.uk

Shelter

An urban & Rural Renaissance:

Planning for the communities of the future

The conclusions of Shelter's national inquiry into housing needs in urban and rural areas.

Deputy Prime Minister, Rt Hon John Prescott said of the report

"...a timely contribution to the crucial debate about where we all live in the new millennium... It recognises the need to ensure that planning and housing policies are interwoven so as to meet the need for good quality affordable homes..."

Shelter's national inquiry into housing shows that potentially too many homes are going to be built for the rich and not enough for the poor. The report is based on extensive evidence gathered by an independent panel in London, Gloucester, Norwich, Stevenage and Newcastle. The panel's recommendations make essential reading for planning departments, environmental groups, builders, tenants and residents groups.

Please send me _____ copies of *An Urban & Rural Renaissance* at £10.00 per set (includes p&p)

☐ I enclose a cheque/postal order (payable to 'Shelter') for £_____

☐ Please debit my Credit/Delta/Switch card

Card No: ☐☐☐☐ ☐☐☐☐ ☐☐☐☐ ☐☐☐☐

Expiry date: ☐☐☐☐   Start date: ☐☐☐☐   Issue No: ☐☐
(Switch/Delta)   (Switch/Delta)

Name: _____

Address:_____

_____

Postcode: _____ Tel: _____

Please photocopy this form and return it to:

Shelter Publications
88 Old Street
London EC1V 9HU
Or fax: 020 7505 2030
Visit Shelter's website at http://www.shelter.org.uk

Shelter

Risks
Home ownership and job insecurity

How is the changing employment market affecting home ownership?

Shelter's new report *Risks* reveals that self-employed and part-time workers are three times more likely than permanent employees to fall into mortgage areas.

Backed by informative statistics and individual case studies, this accessible report examines the growth in all insecure forms of employment and considers what can be done to help home owners keep up with their mortgage repayments.

Suggestions on how to minimise risk for future home owners make vital reading for all policy-makers, mortgage lenders, home owners and advisers.

Please send me _____ copies of *Risks* at £9.25 (includes p&p)

Special offer: deduct 10% if you are ordering 5 or more copies

☐ I enclose a cheque/postal order (payable to 'Shelter') for £_____

☐ Please debit my Credit/Delta/Switch card

Card No: ☐☐☐☐ ☐☐☐☐ ☐☐☐☐ ☐☐☐☐

Expiry date: ☐☐☐☐   Start date: ☐☐☐☐   Issue No: ☐☐
(Switch/Delta)   (Switch/Delta)

Name: _____

Address:_____

_____

Postcode: _____ Tel: _____

Please photocopy this form and return it to:
Shelter Publications
88 Old Street
London EC1V 9HU
Or fax: 020 7505 2030
Visit Shelter's website at http://www.shelter.org.uk

Shelter

Shelter

Guide to Housing Benefit and Council Tax Benefit 1999-00

John Zebedee & Martin Ward

New Edition

This guide has been completely updated to describe the housing benefit and council tax benefit schemes from April 1999. Full of practical examples and useful tables it covers the following and much more.

- the new rules about contrived lettings and other cases in which HB cannot be awarded
- recent changes about child care charges
- who can get HB and CTB (including second adult rebate)
- the impact of the New Deal and Welfare to Work
- how much rent is taken into account in all types of tenure
- dealing with absences, moving home and HB on two homes
- discretionary provisions for avoiding exceptional hardship.

Please send me......... copy(ies) of the Guide to Housing Benefit and Council Tax Benefit 1999-00 at £18.45 (including P&P)

Name _____

Address _____

_____ Postcode _____

I enclose a cheque for £ _____ payable to Shelter/please debit my credit card

Card No. _____

Issue No _____ Valid from _____ (for Delta or Switch) Expiry Date _____

Please return to Shelter Publications, 88 Old Street, London EC1V 9HU.
Tel: 0171 505 2043. Fax 0171 505 2167

Buy a Shelter publication and help a homeless person.

Registered company 1038133. Registered charity 263710. VAT No. 626555624

G